Charlee Swanson

American
Born Jersey City NJ
1945

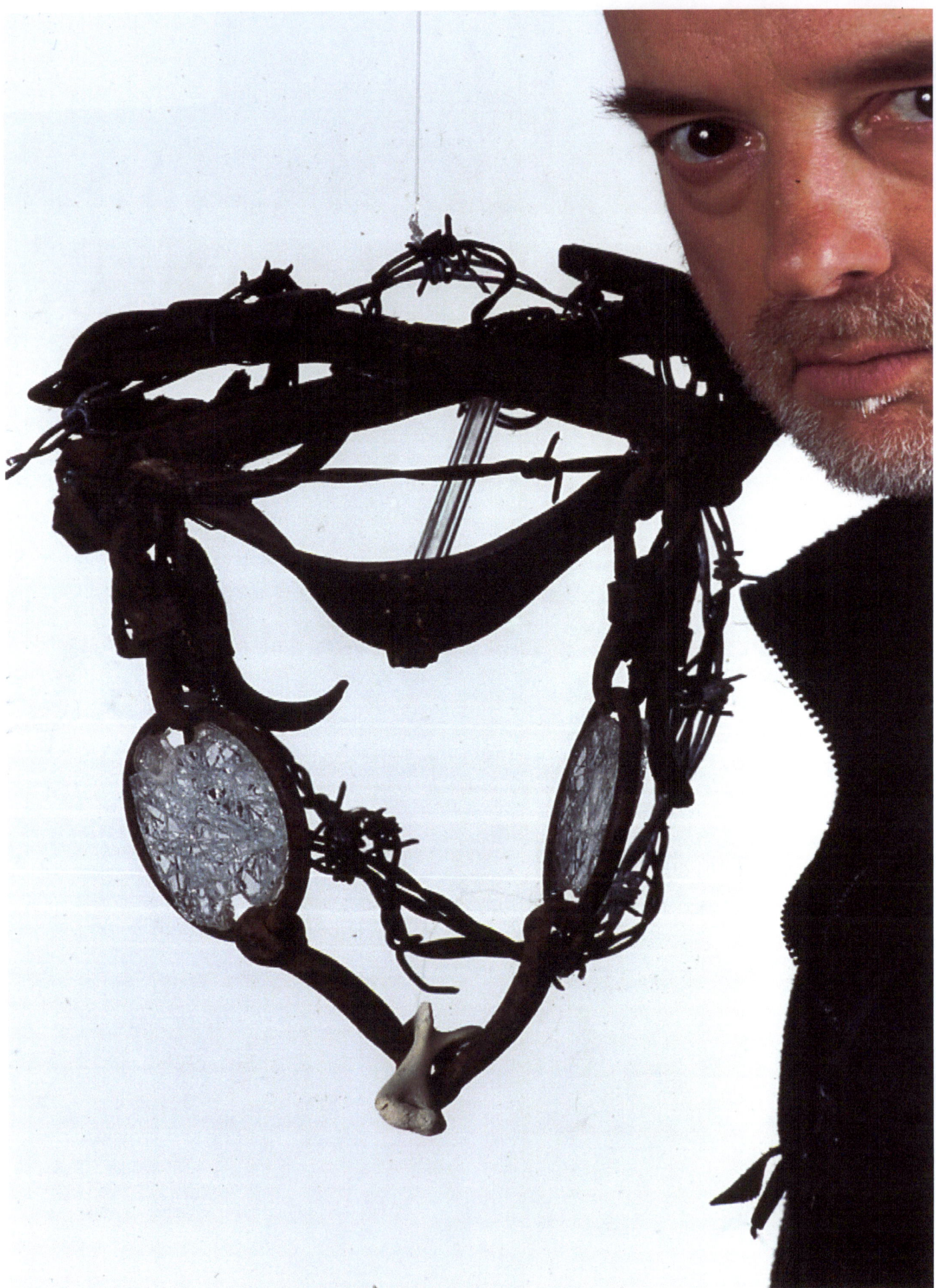

Artist
Statement

My work is about the materials.

I use broken glass and steel; discarded materials from glass shops, metal fabricators, and scrap-yards. I refuse to use traditional methods of art making.

I prefer industrial discards and supplies. Recycling and reusing these materials, I assign them a new meaning. I see this as a form of alchemy.

Viewers have been conditioned to respond to glass and steel as objects of support, protection, and construction. By re-contextualizing these materials, I confront and engage the viewer.

I use torches, grinders, and hammers to scar, mar, and manipulate the surface of steel. I cultivate rust using time, elements, and weather to make images appear.

I draw in glass by breaking it with tools and techniques I developed. I use light and shadows to project images.

A recent body of work comes from my concept of accidental energy: a force of misfortune that transforms the guard rails of our highways into twisted, bent, and tangled shapes. I select, manipulate, and combine these forms to create sculptures.

Currently I focus on grids, cubes, movements, and suspension. I'm working with industrial steel shelving baskets that I salvaged from a factory that was being demolished.

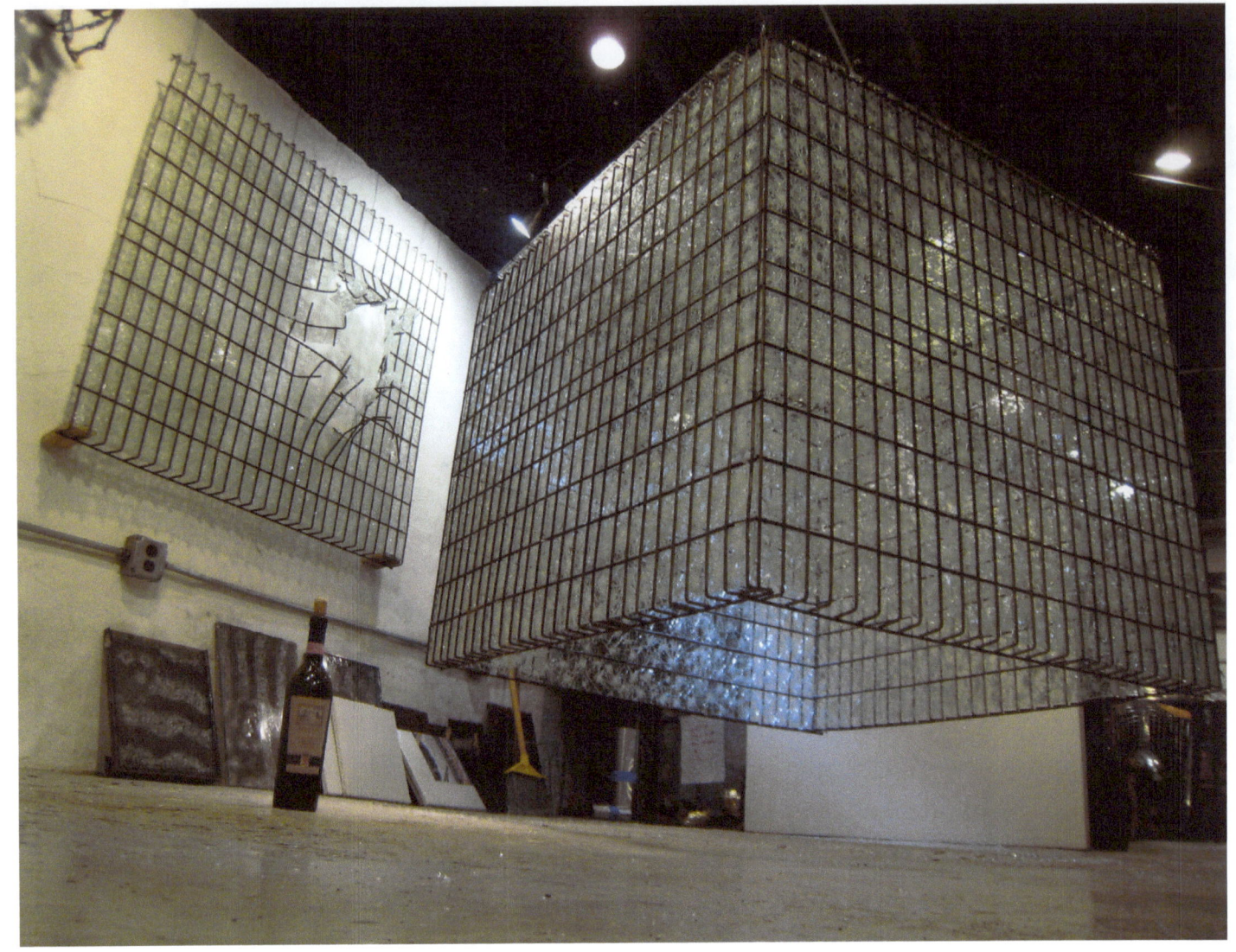

Cube Project

The cubes are modular; all vertical sides are interchangeable and can be configured in many ways. These modular parts can function as walls dividing a space, or as an open-sided cube, inviting the viewer into the space they define.

"Breaking Out" works as a relief when suspended from the ceiling and a few inches away from the wall, or as part of the Cube, Breaking Out Of the Box. The flexibility of this new work allows me to create site-specific installations to confront and engage the viewer.

The Cube can be suspended in a kinetic installation, rotating on a swivel, allowing the viewer to experience the

illusion of the surfaces changing from rust to broken glass and back as it rotates.

This can be experienced by visiting my website, www.charleeswanson.com. Go to "Gallery", click "Cube", and scroll down to "Cube In Motion" (video).

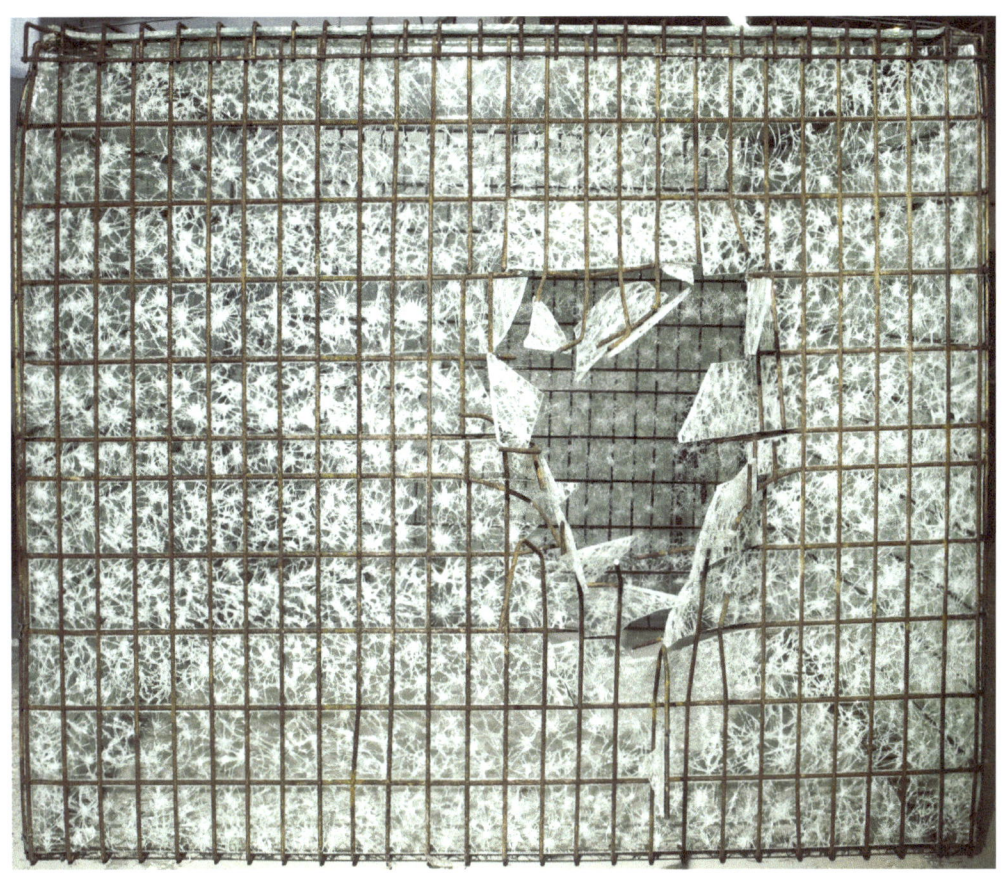

Detail Breaking Out on Cube

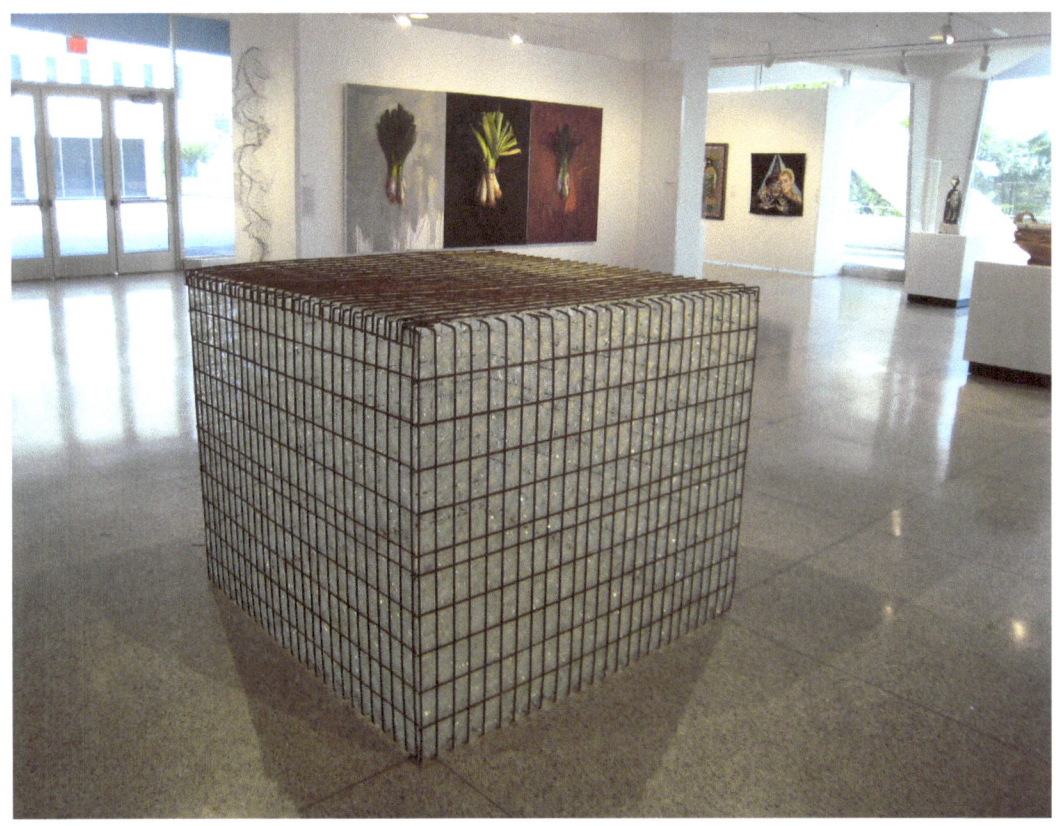

Cube at NJ State Museum Fine Arts Annual

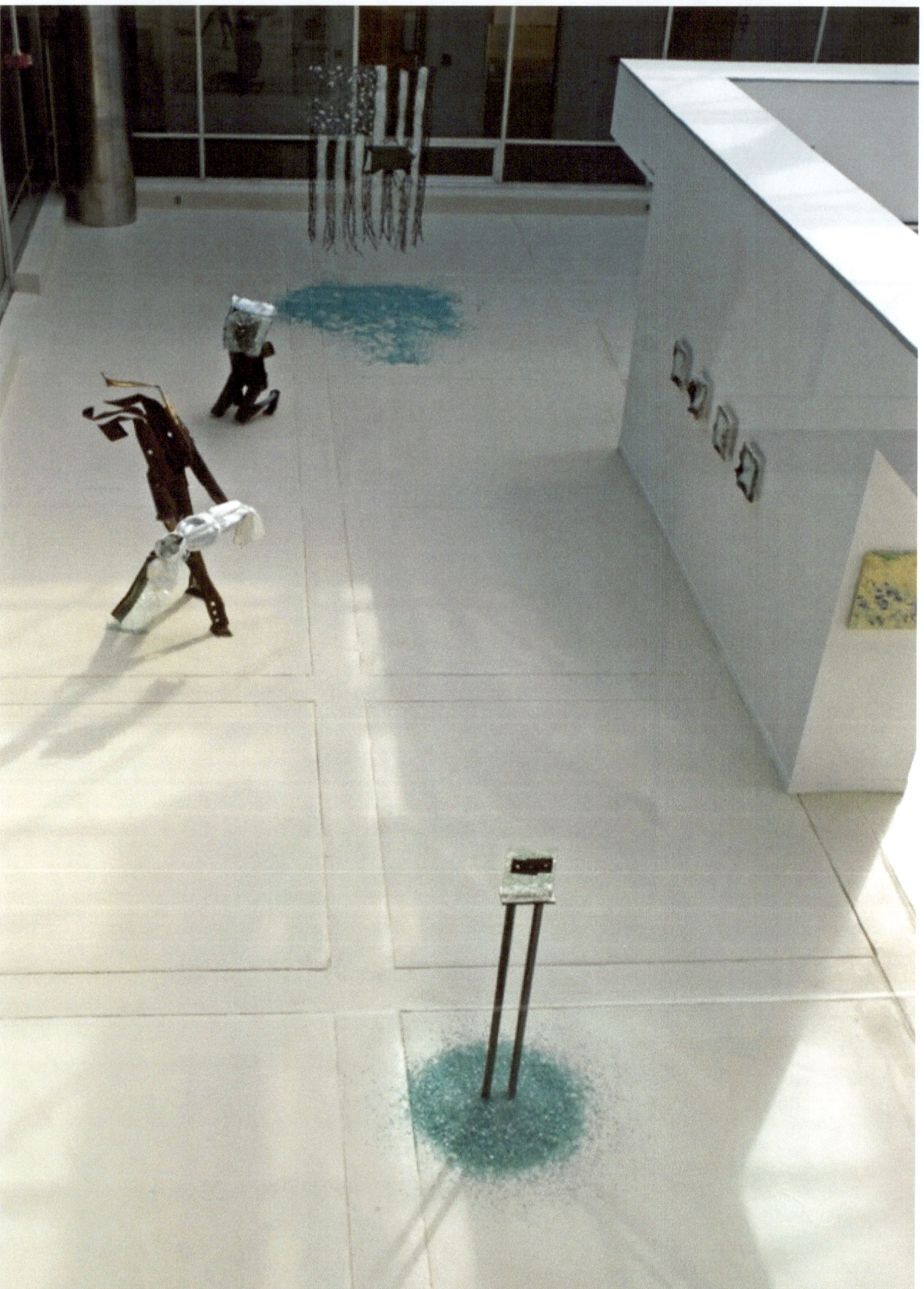

The Horrors of War

This installation was done at William Paterson University.

It incorporates Eyes of Deception (foreground), War Baby, War Torture, the large flag Destruction, and four Burned and Broken canvases (on wall).

Eyes of Deception represents what led us into a never-ending war. War Baby and War Torture depict the horror of war, while the flag hangs at the rear, signifying the destruction. The four Burned and Broken canvases on the wall are the windows through which the world watches in horror.

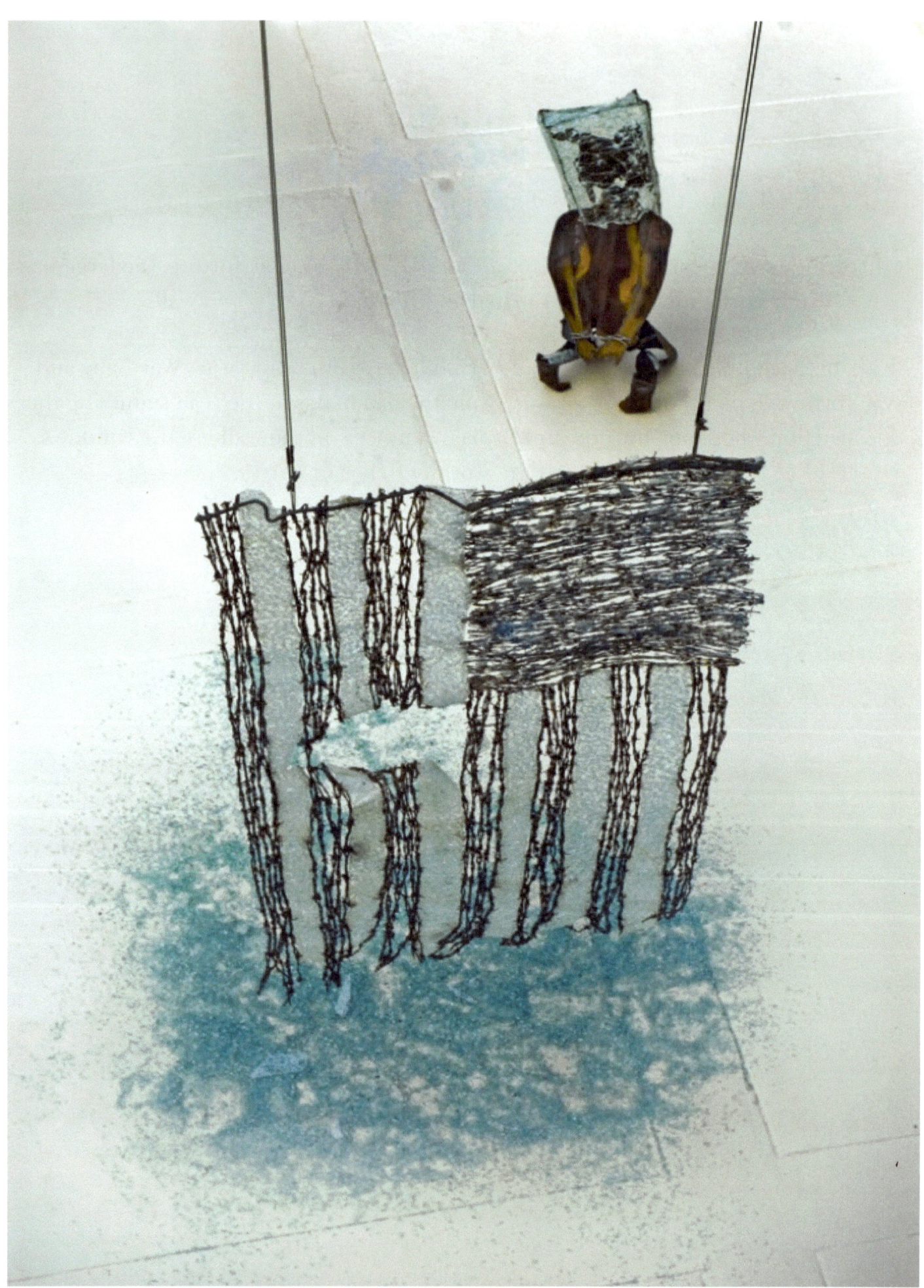

War Torture

War Torture is 4' x 2' x 3'
Broken glass, barbed wire, & accidental metal

Destruction

Destruction (Flag) 4' x 6' x 1'
Broken glass & barbed wire
It is suspended on steel cable, with broken
glass on the floor beneath it.

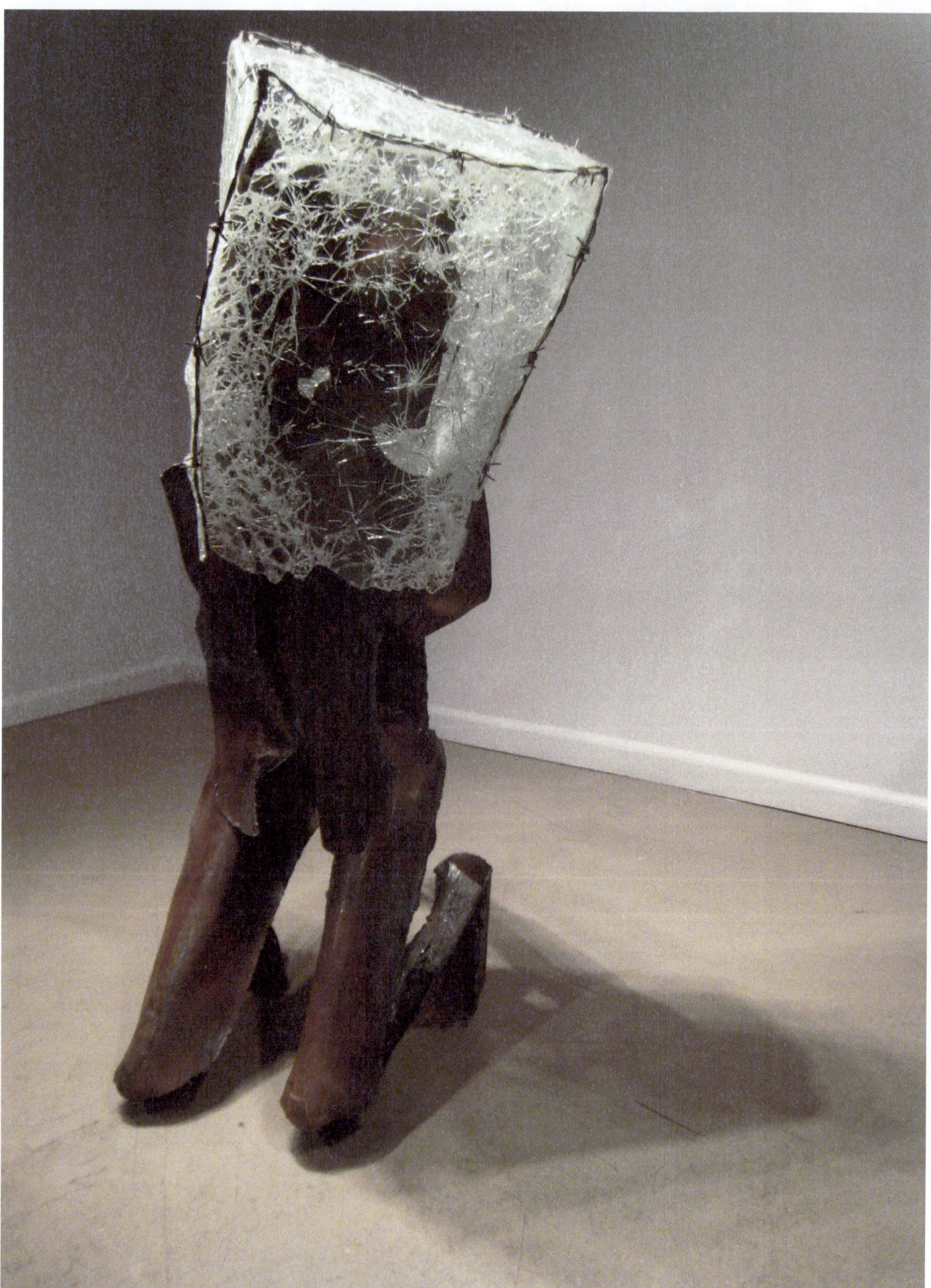

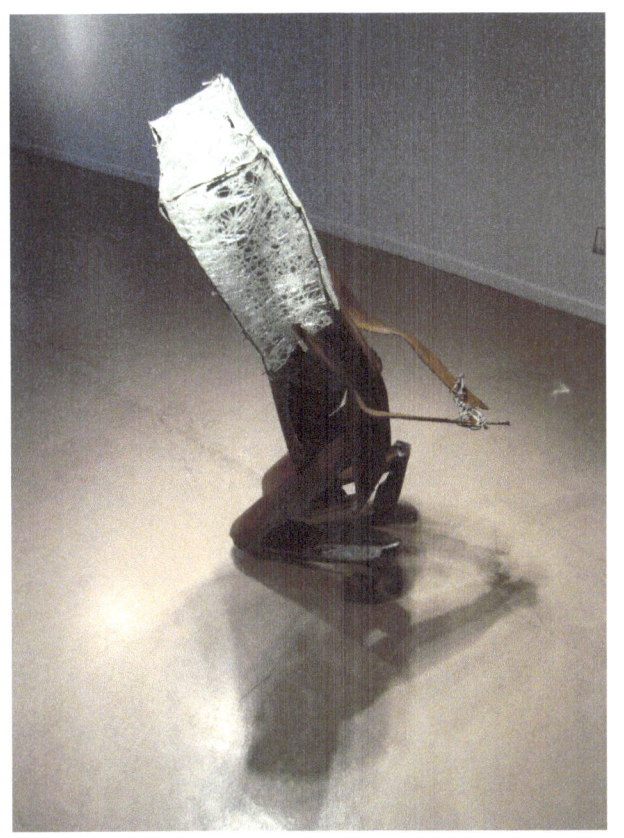
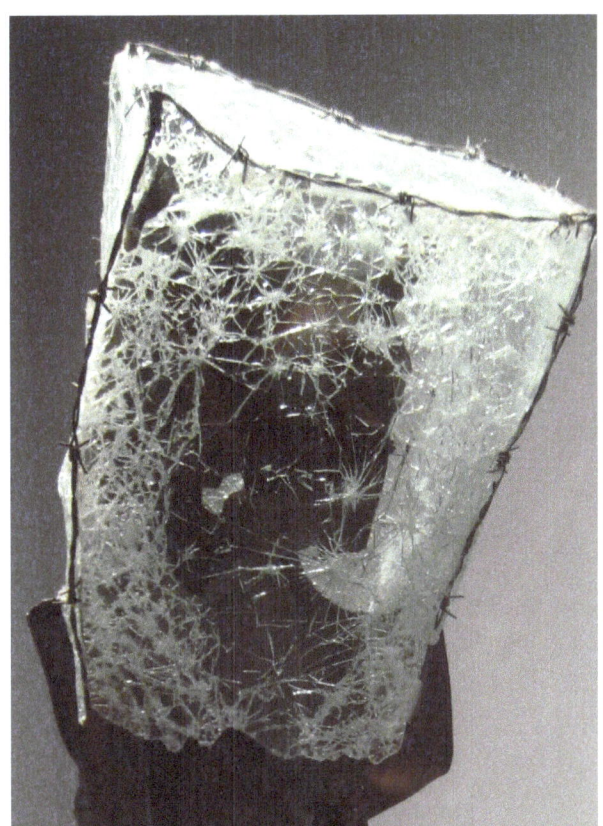
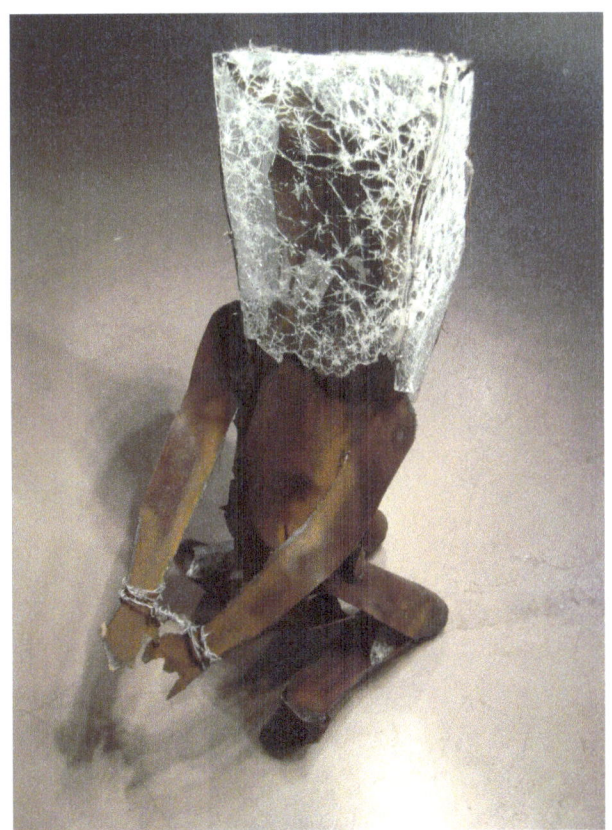
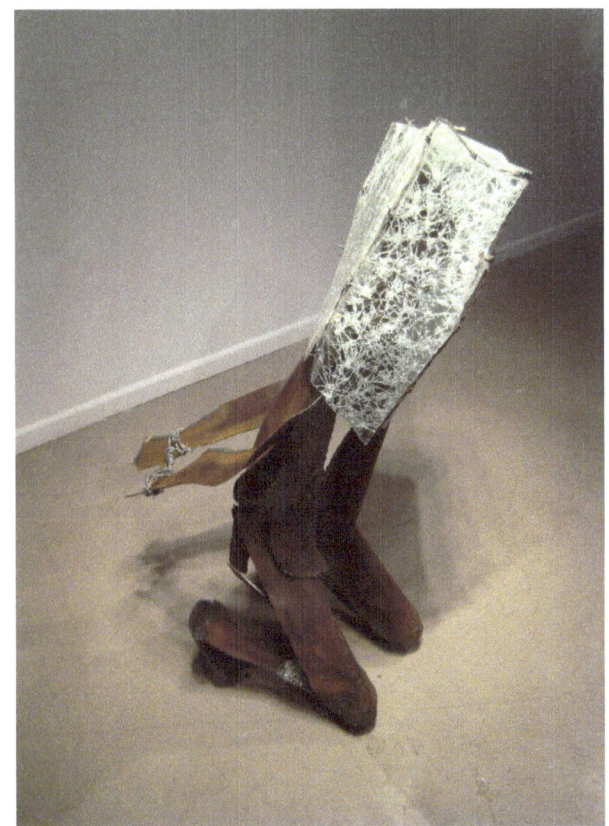

War Torture
City Without Walls

approximately 4' x 2' x 3'
Accidental metal, broken glass, & barbed wire.

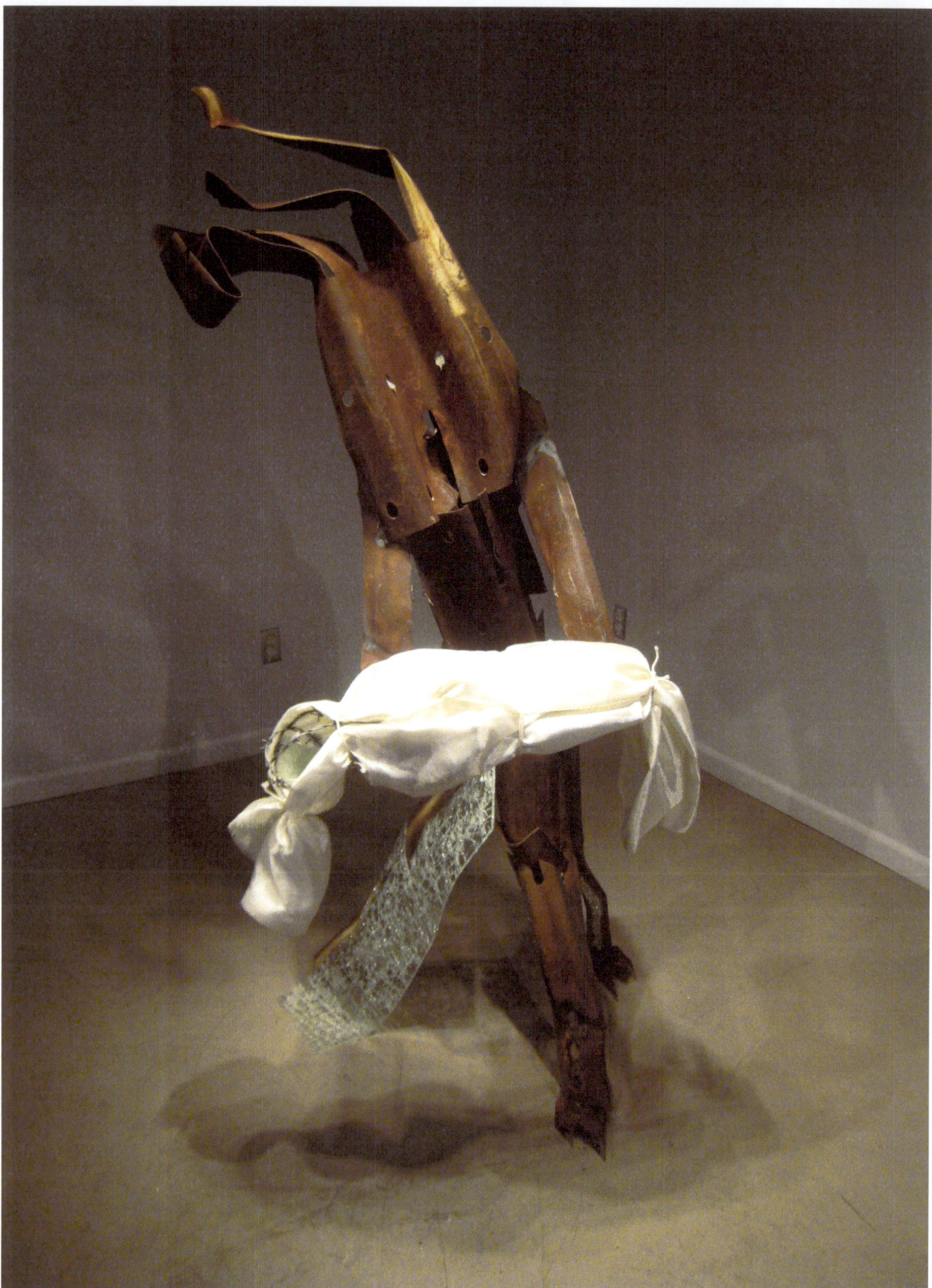

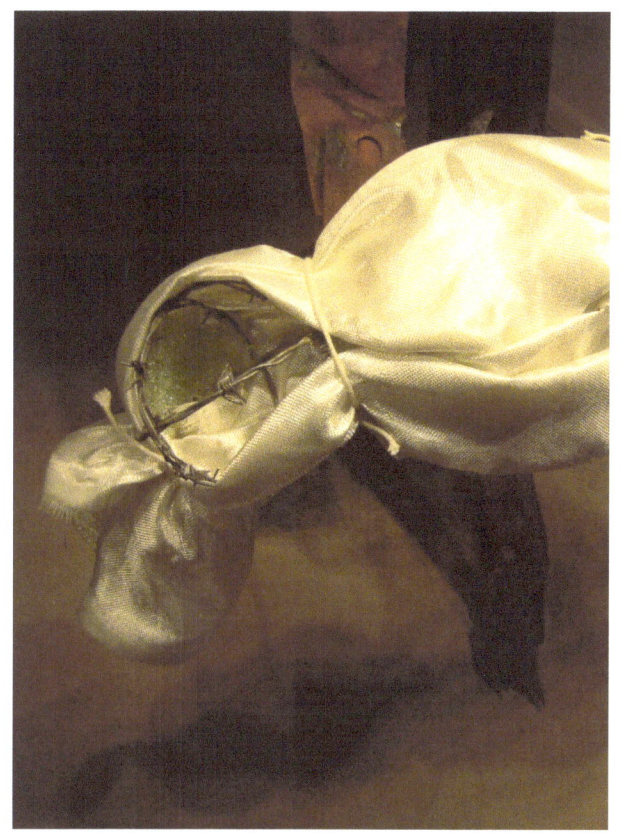
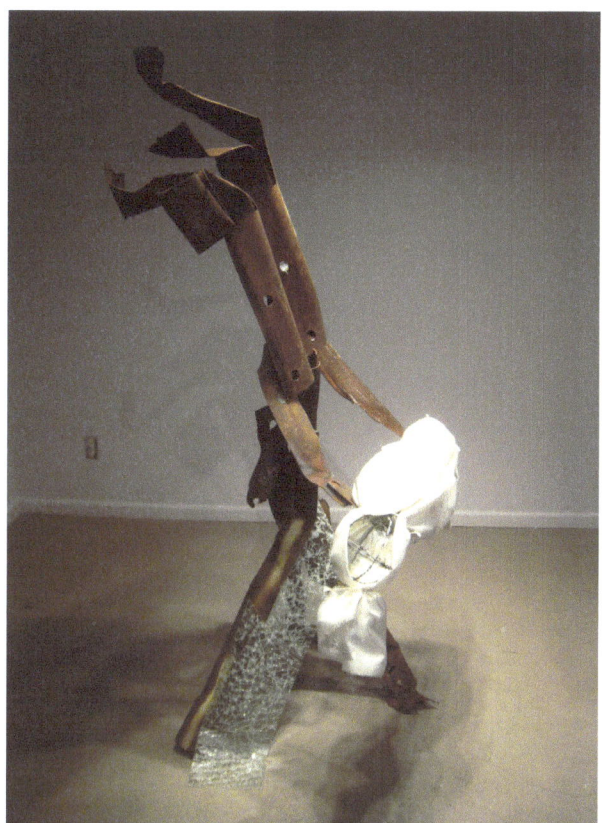
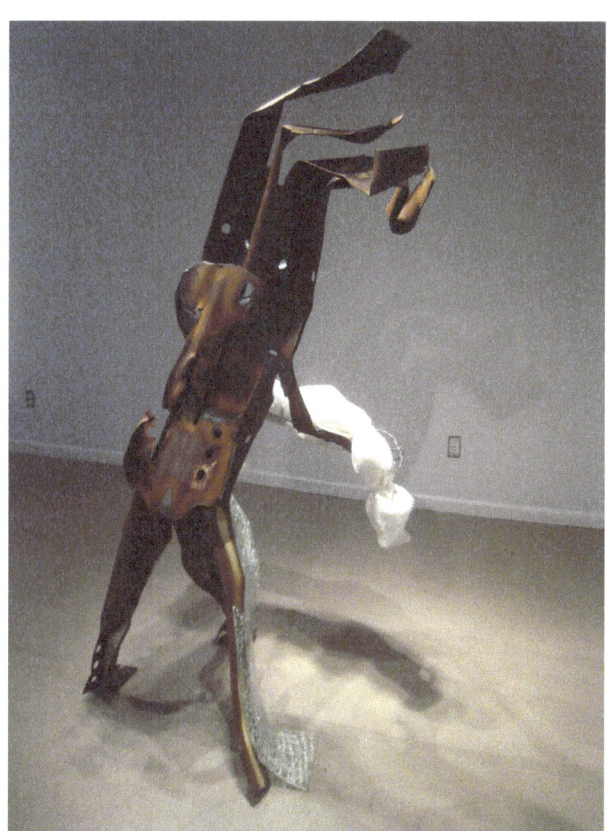
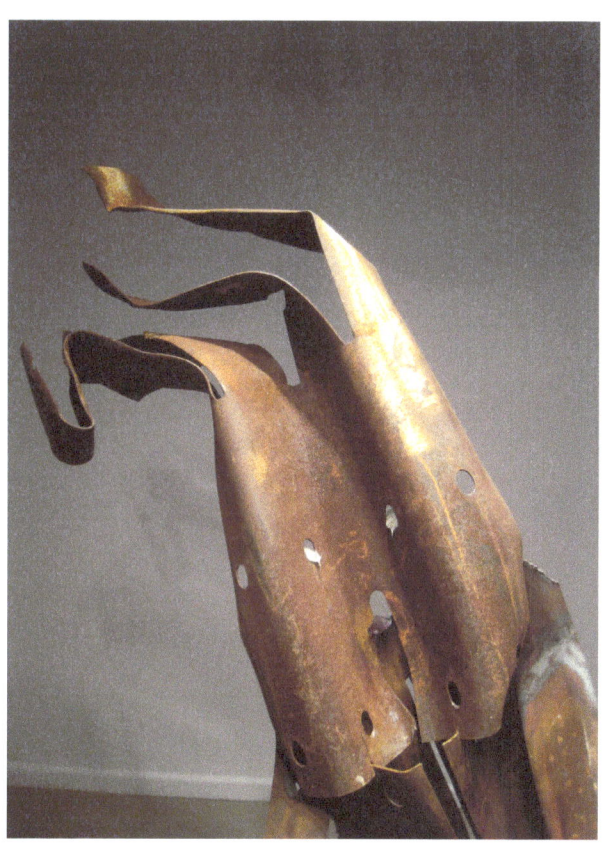

War Baby
City Without Walls

Approximately 6' x 4' x 3'

Accidental metal, broken glass, barbed wire & fiberglass cloth.

Accidental Metal Installation at Long Branch, NJ 2007

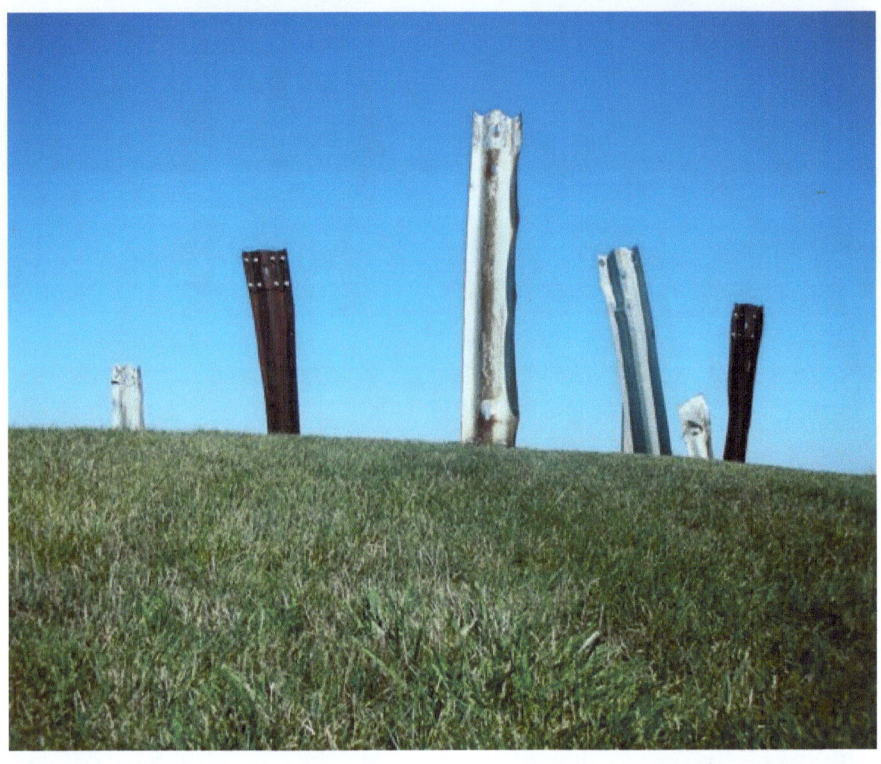

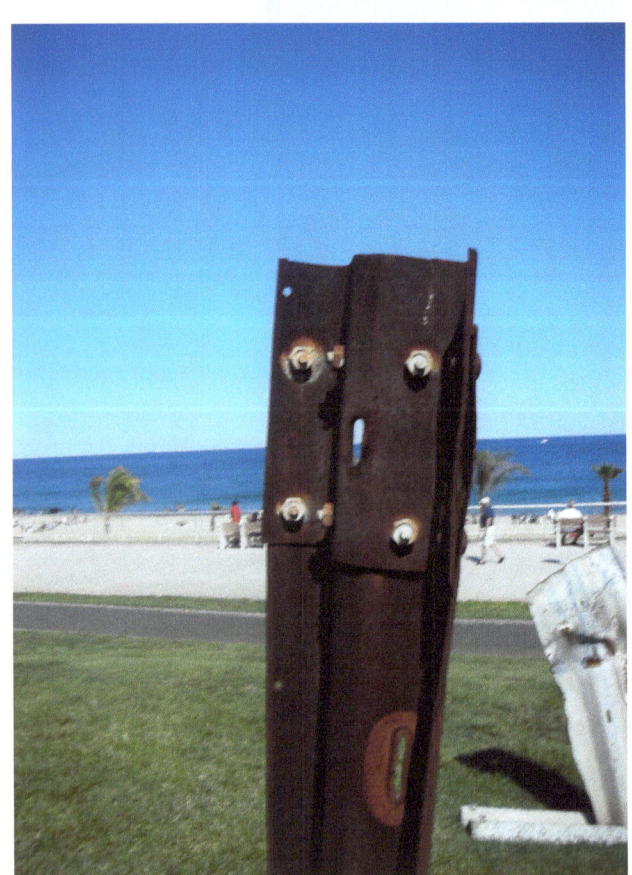

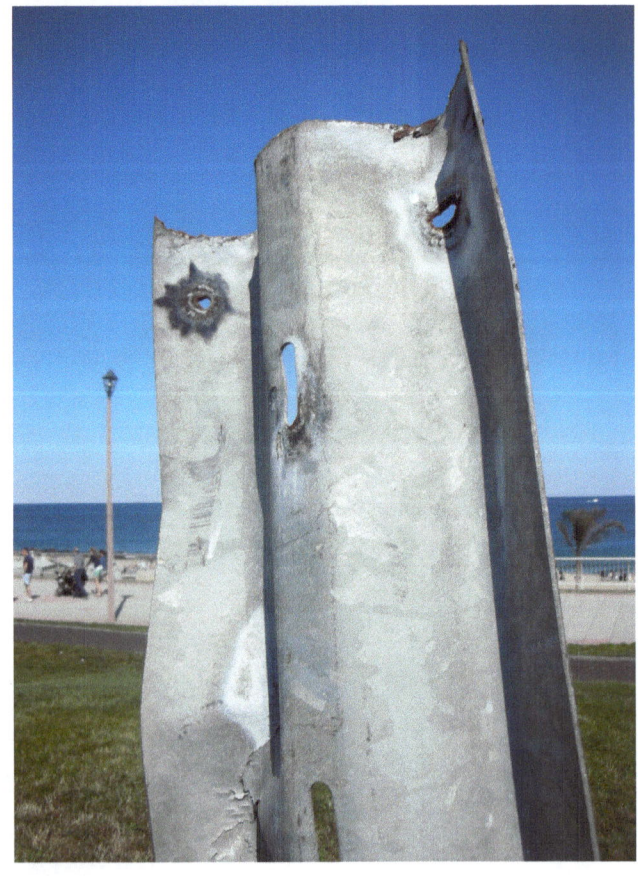

Above Accidental Metal Installation
Below & Opposite Details
Galvanized & core 10 steel (dimensions are variable)

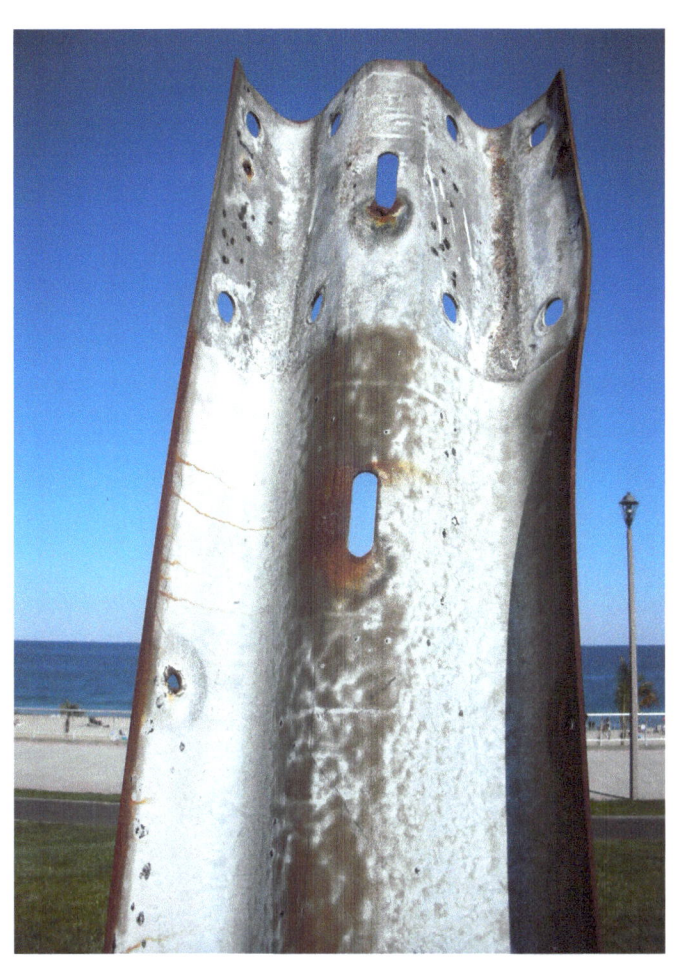
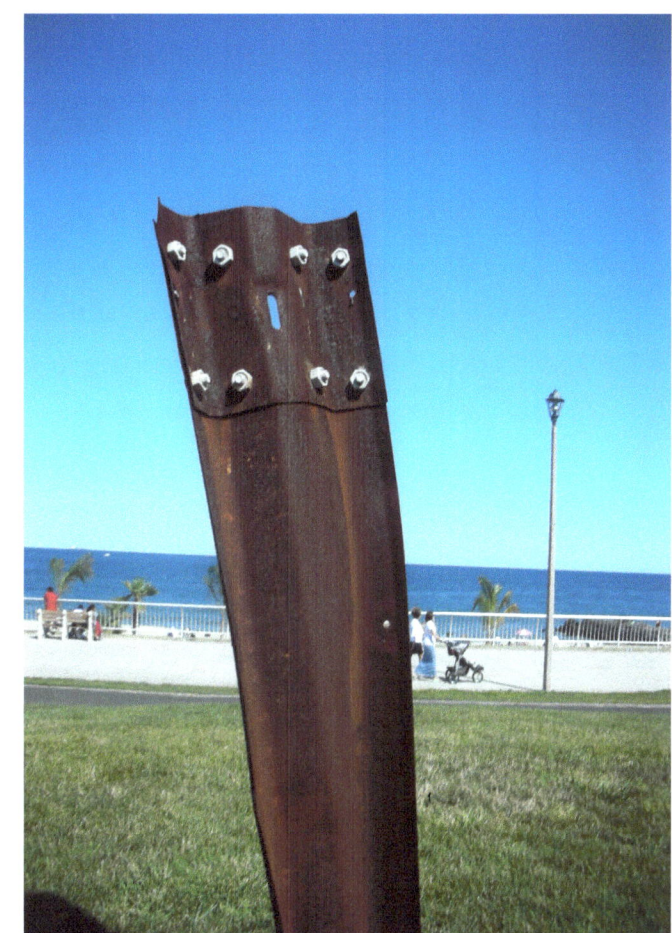
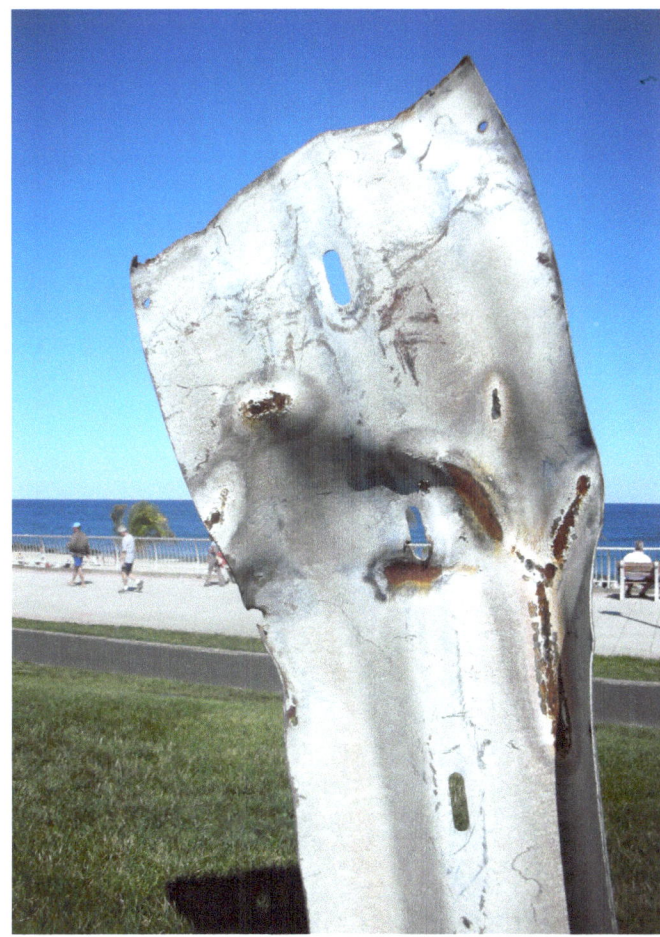
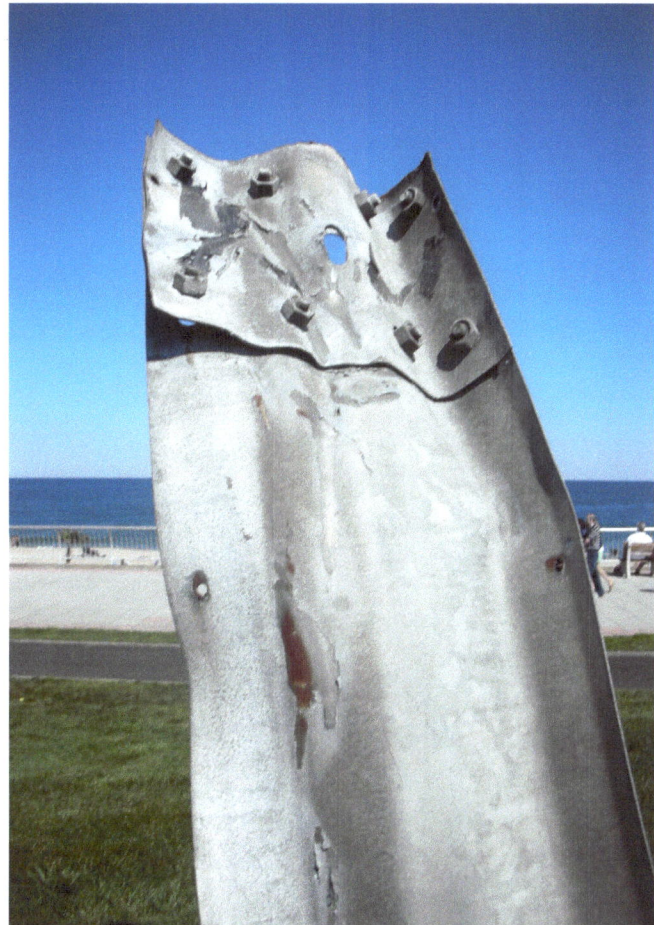

Works on Paper

Primitive Prints
Soot Works
Rust Crayon Drawings

I print with scraps of metal, make rust crayons with steel, sawdust, and draw by making marks with acetylene soot.

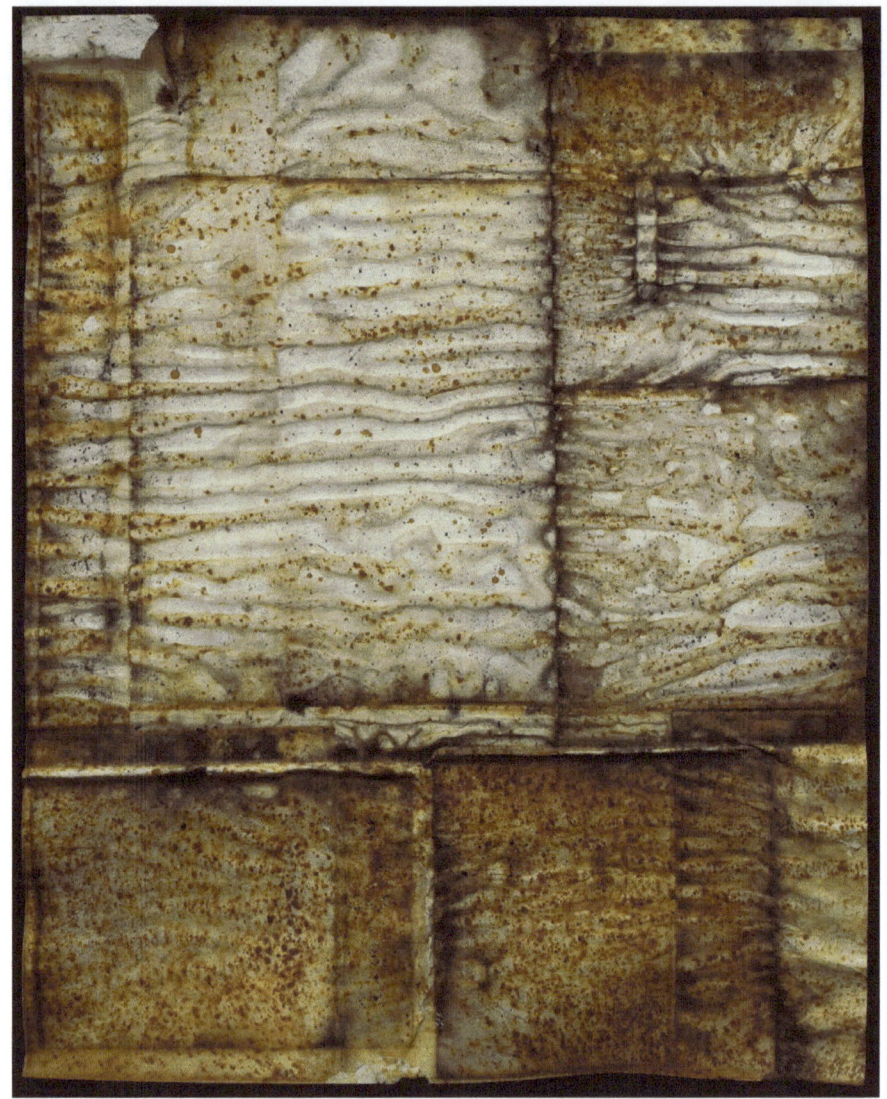

Primitive Prints

Above and Opposite Primitive Prints
A steel workbench is the bed of my primitive printing press. Steel plates are intentionally scarred and rusted, then arranged and indexed to the paper. Time, nature, rain, and composted dirt are used to make the prints. (dimensions are variable)

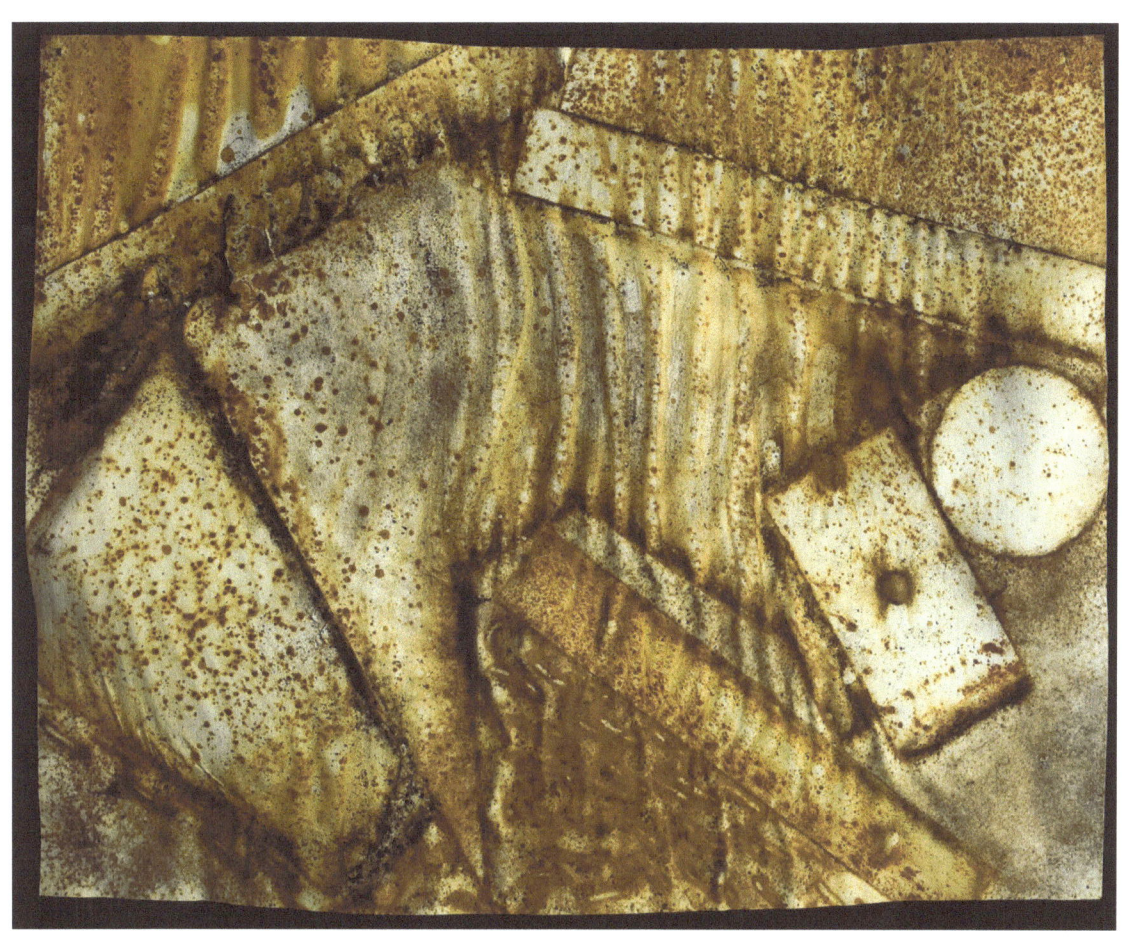

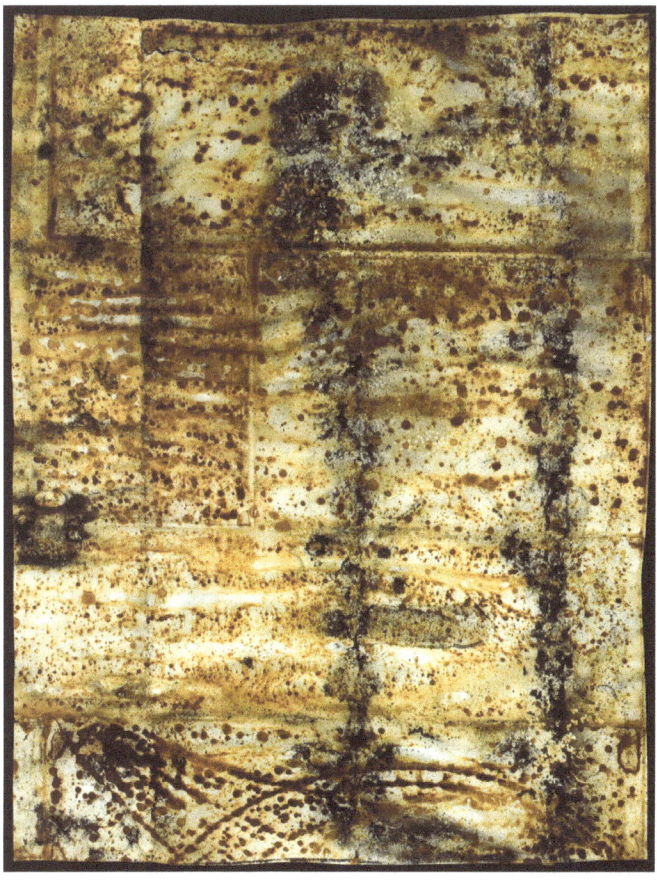

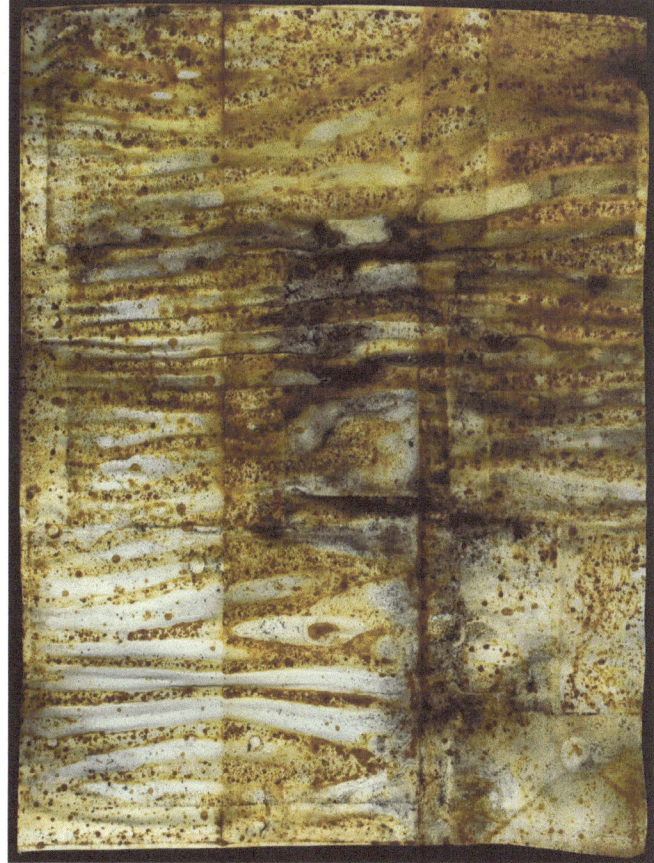

Soot Works

My soot works are drawings made with the soot from my oxyacetylene torch. The mind tells the hand what to do, but the moment the soot leaves the tip of the torch, the anticipation begins, wondering if it will land as planned. It's over in seconds.

Below & Opposite Soot Works, approx. 12" x 12"
Acetylene soot & paper

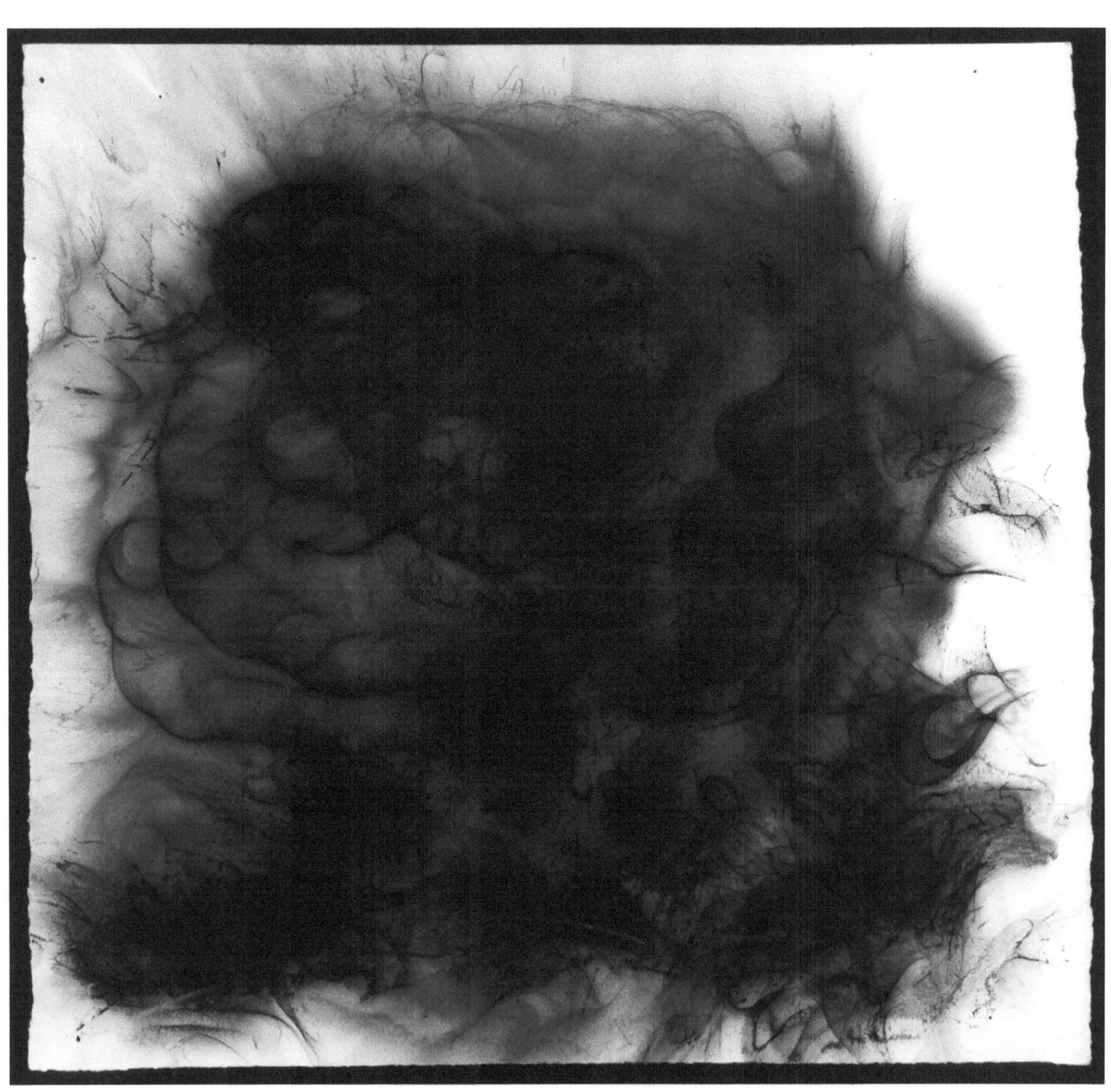

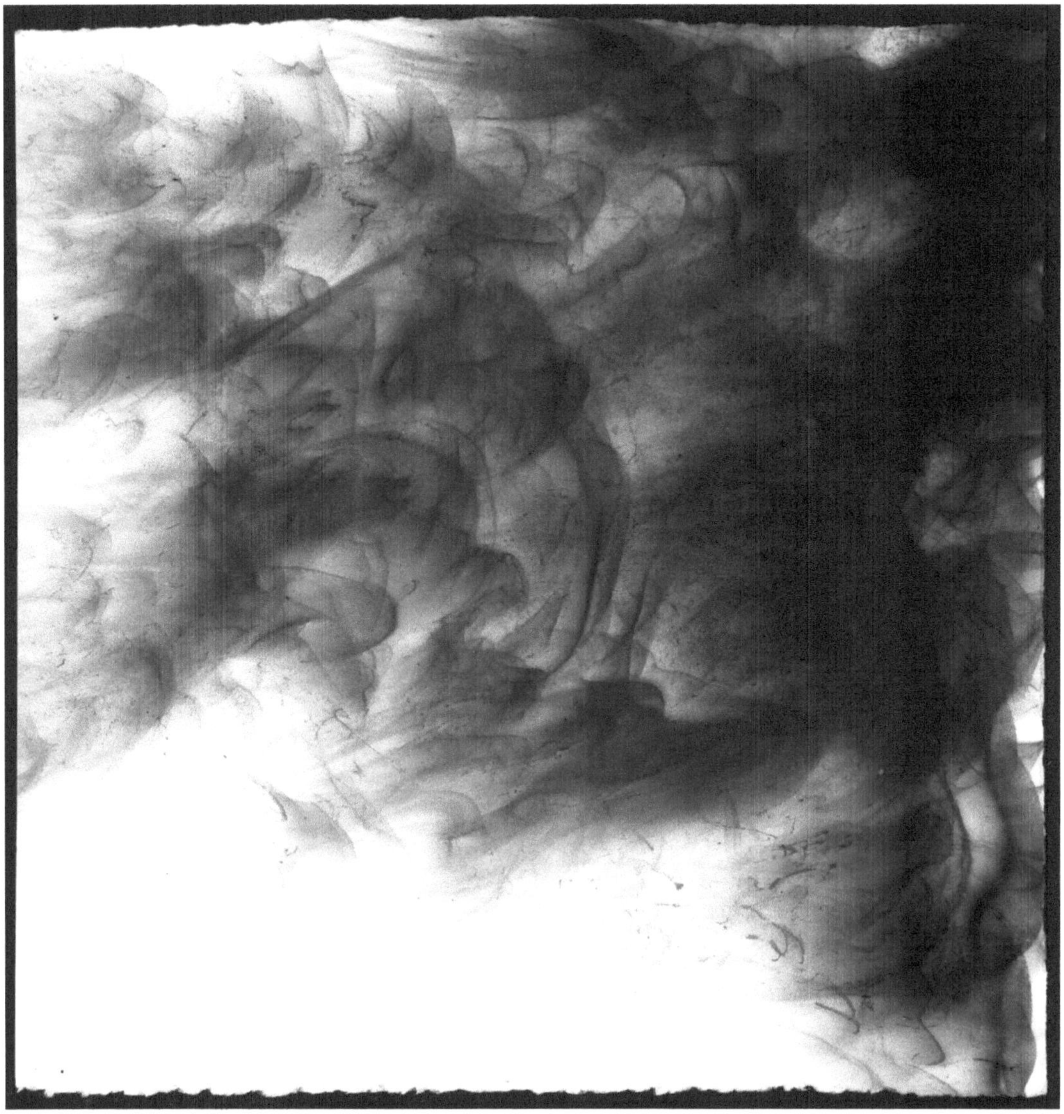

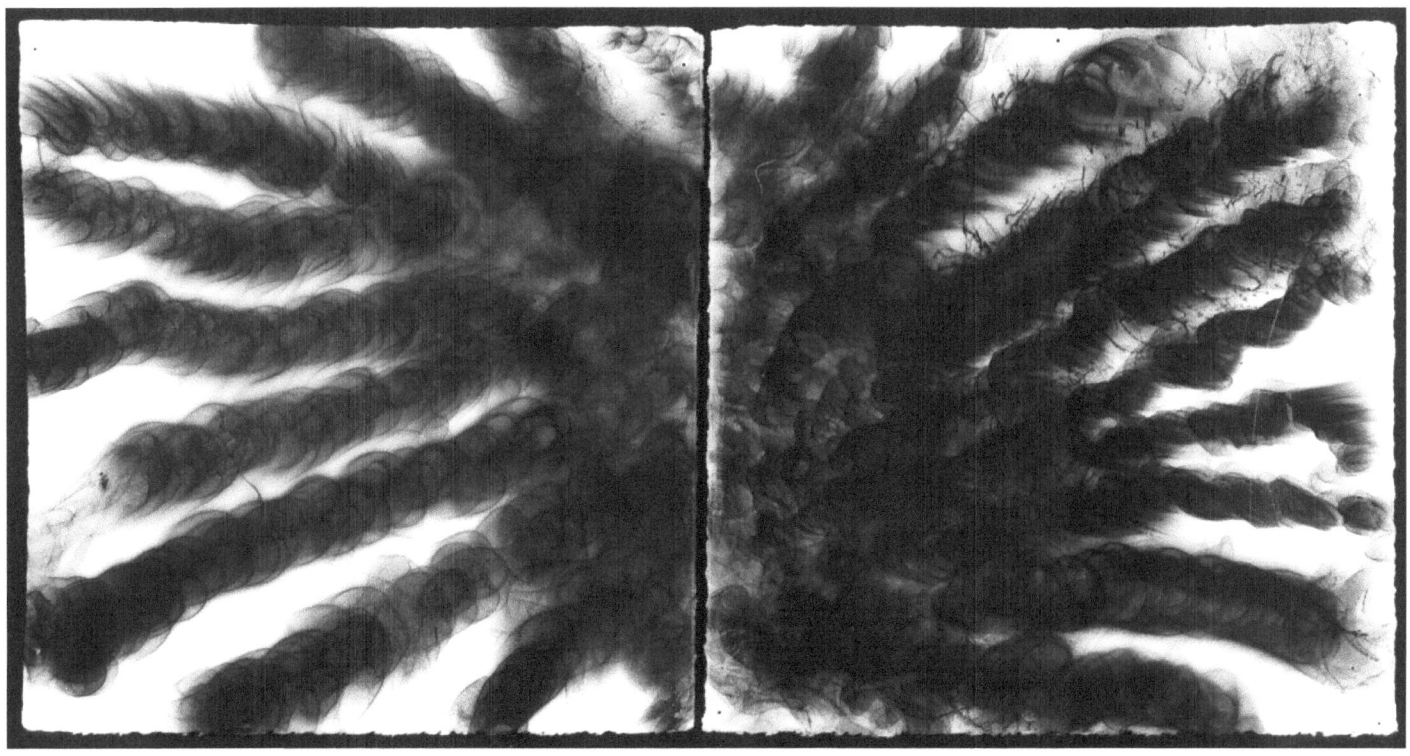

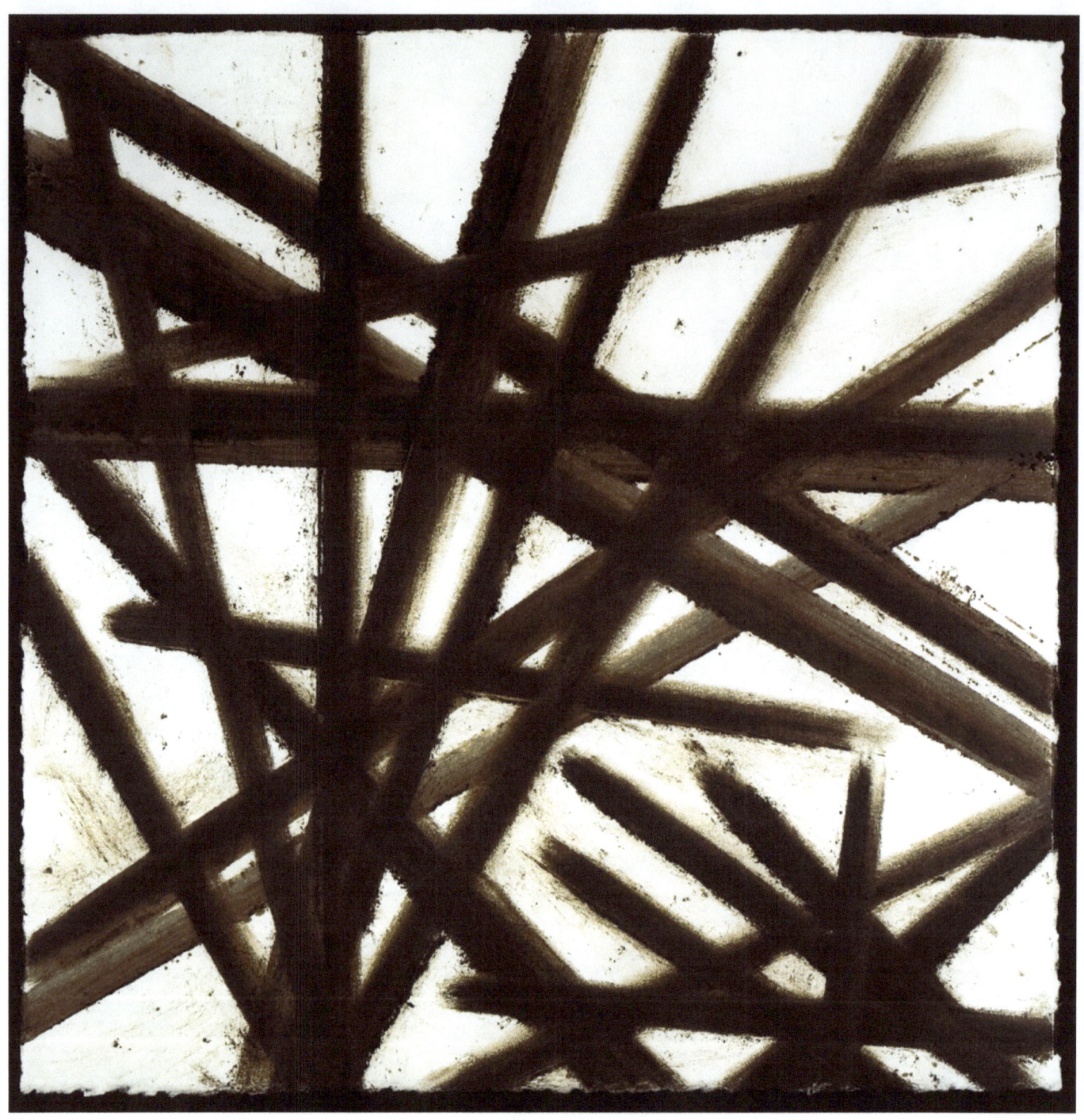

Rust Crayon Drawings

These drawings are an experiment in pushing the limits of my materials.
Rust crayons are made from steel sawdust, harvested from machine shops.
I cultivate the rust and form them into crayons.

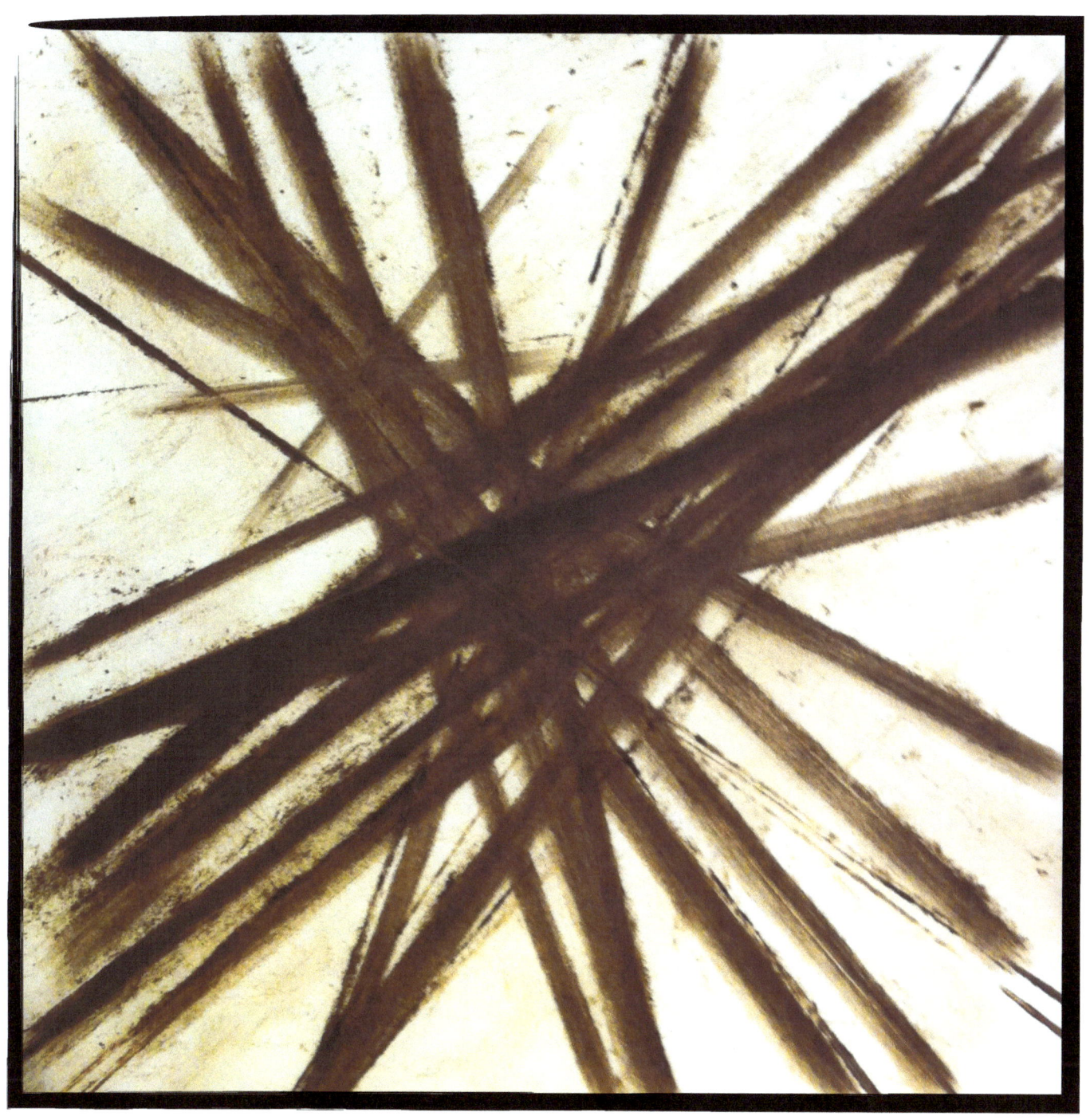

Rust Crayon Drawings,
approx.. 12” x 12”
Rust crayon & paper

American Landscape Series

This series was a departure from a previous body of work, in broken glass and barbed wire, that was figurative and volumetric.

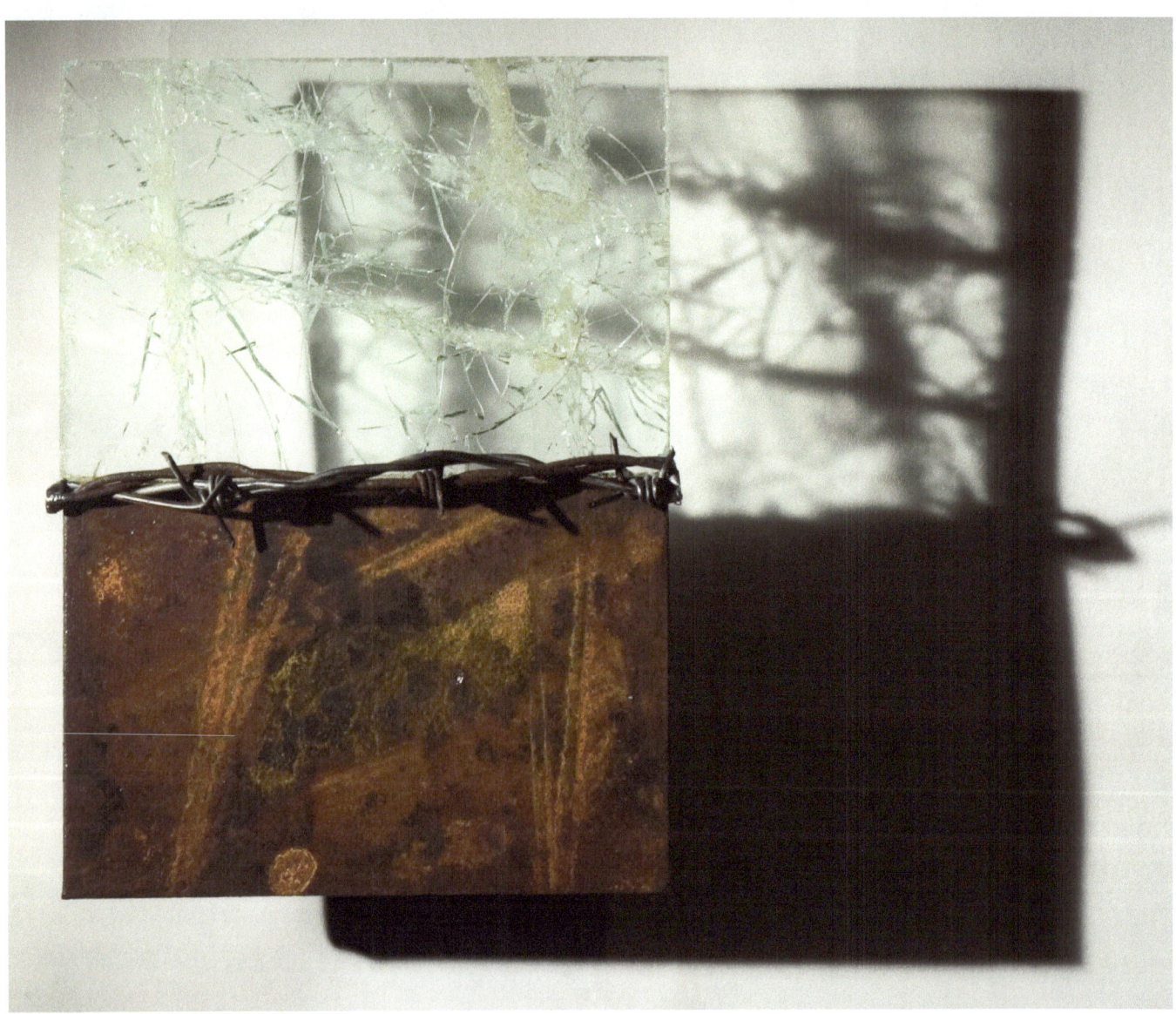

Above: #10, 9" x 7" x 2.5" Broken glass, steel, & barbed wire

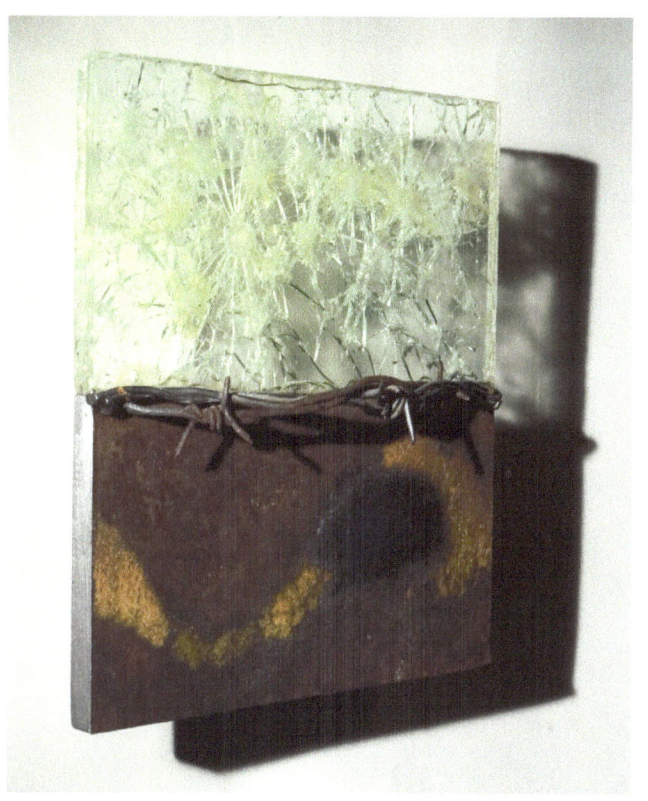
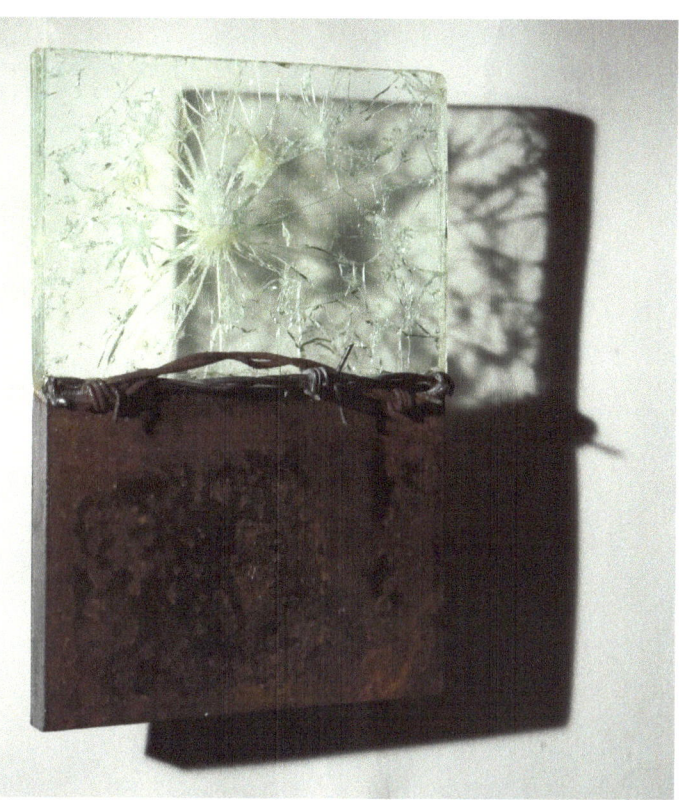
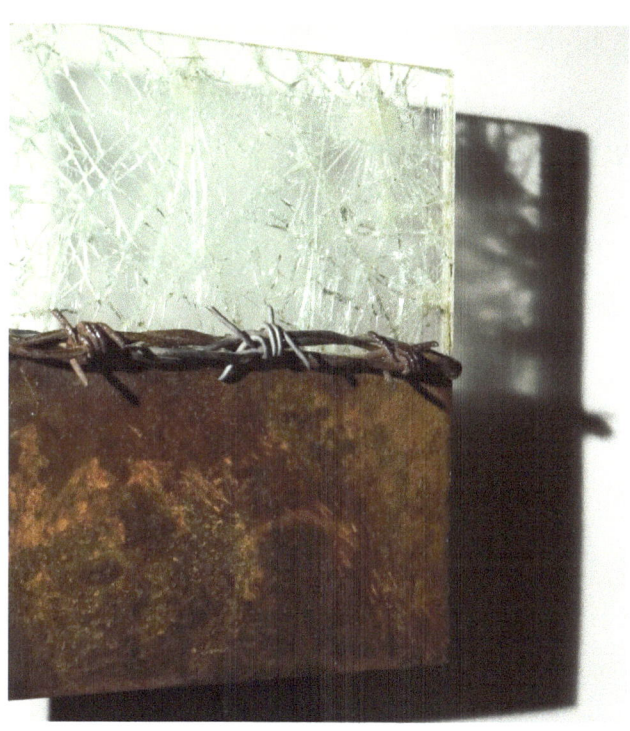
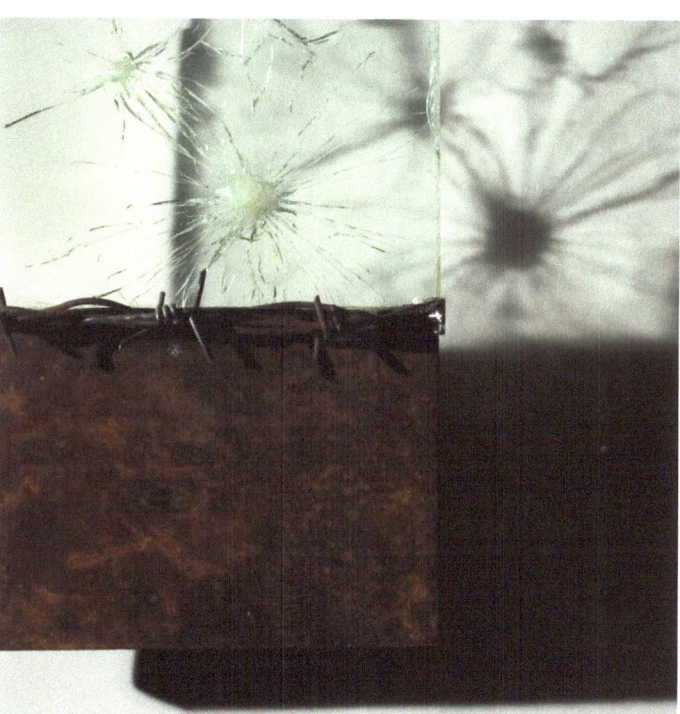

Above (left): #9, approx. 6" x 9" x 2.5", broken glass, steel, & barbed wire

Above (right): #7, approx. 6" x 9" x 2.5", broken glass, steel, & barbed wire

Below (left): #12, approx. 6" x 9" x 2.5", broken glass, steel, & barbed wire

Below (right): #11, approx. 6" x 9" x 2.5", broken glass, steel, & barbed wire

American Landscape Series

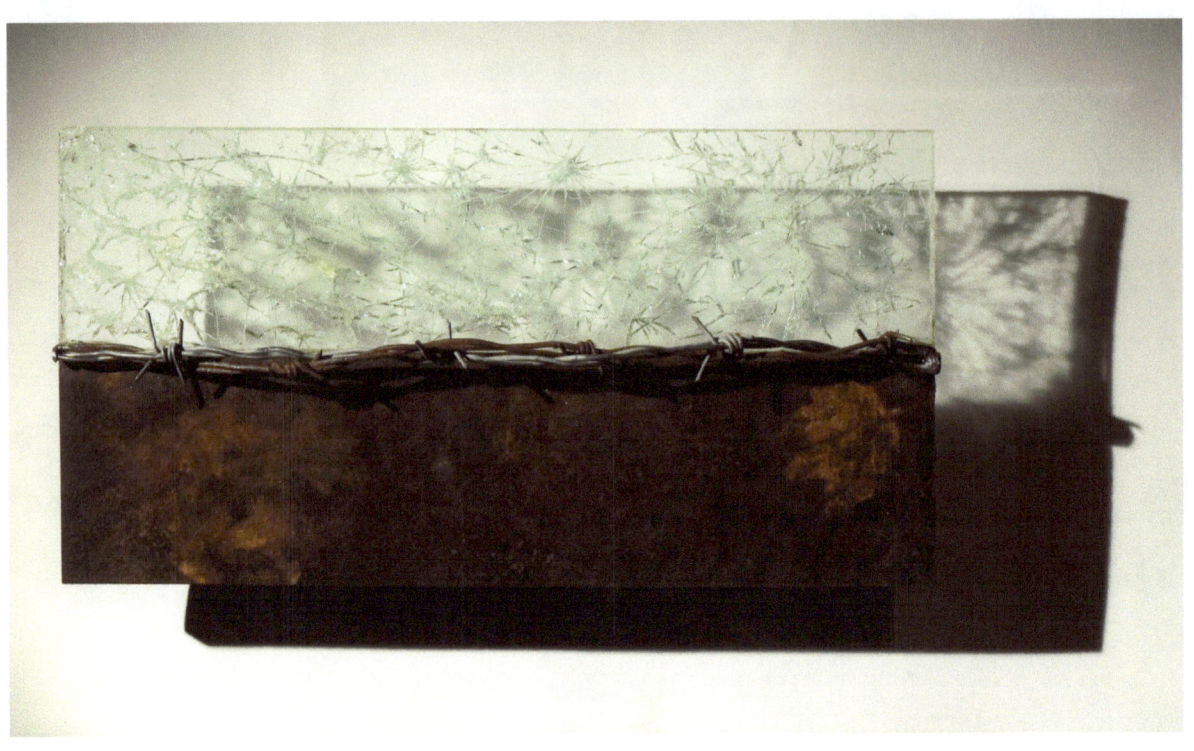

Above: American Landscape #6, 8" x 15.25" x 2.5"
broken glass, steel, & barbed wire

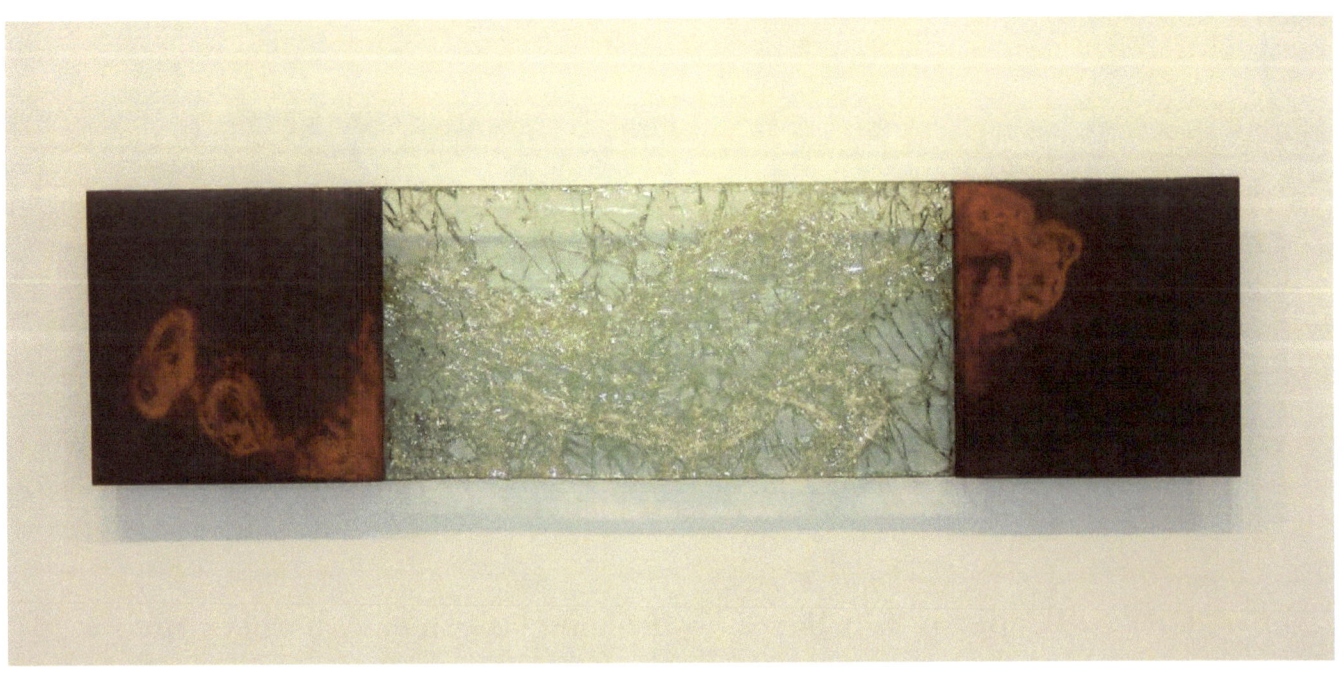

Above: Organic Triptych, 9.5" x 29.5" x 2.5"
broken glass & steel

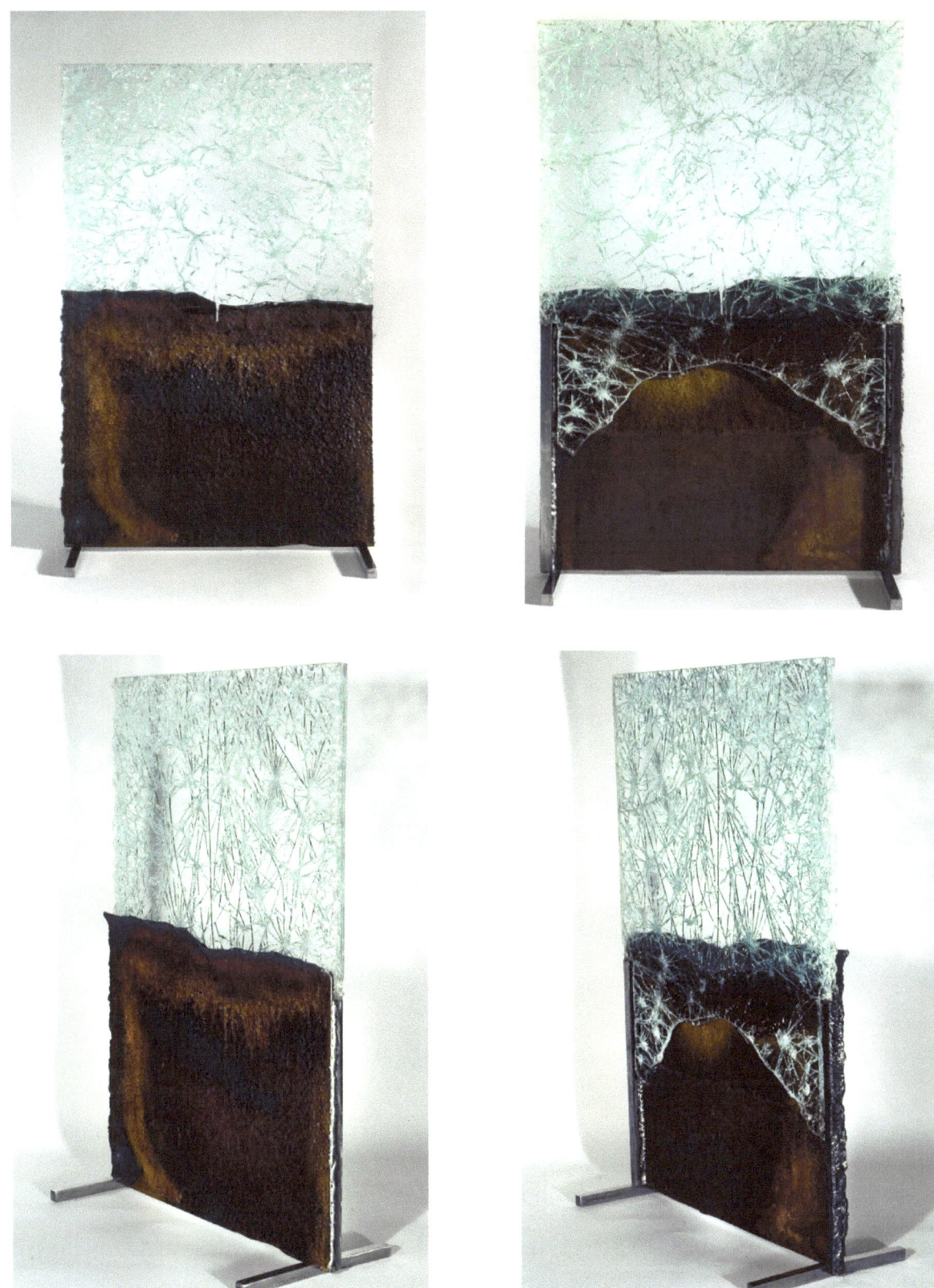

American Landscape #13, 20" x 24" x 8", broken glass & steel
Top Left: detail (front) Top Right: detail (rear)
Bottom Left: detail (side and front) Bottom Right: detail (side and rear)

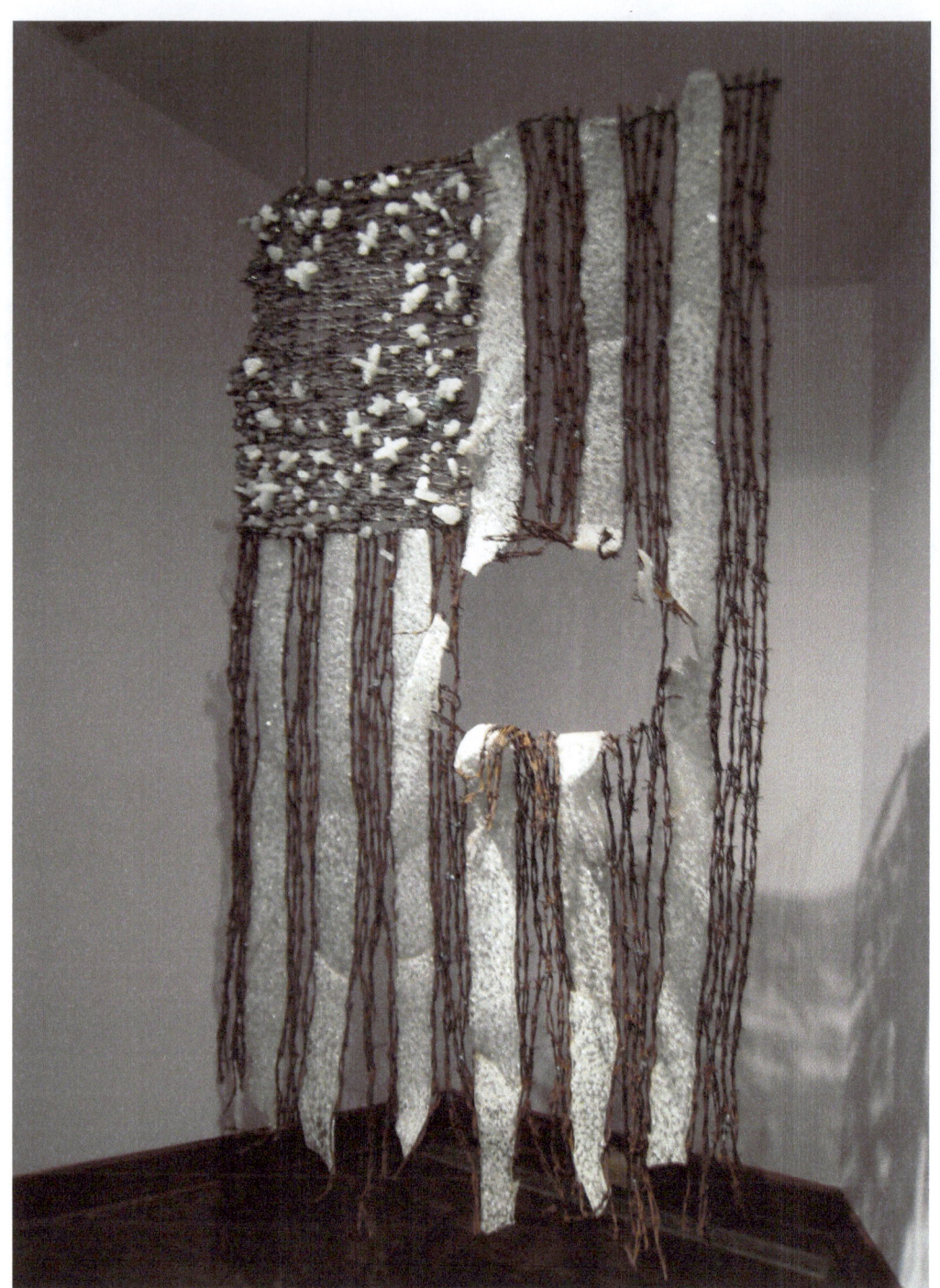

Flag Series

After 9/11, I was deeply moved. For weeks, I meditated, watching smoke plume from the Manhattan skyline. Flag Series (left and opposite page) was a reaction to the death and destruction that occurred that day.

Above: Destruction, at the Allentown Art Museum.
6' 8" x 4' x 14" broken glass & barbed wire

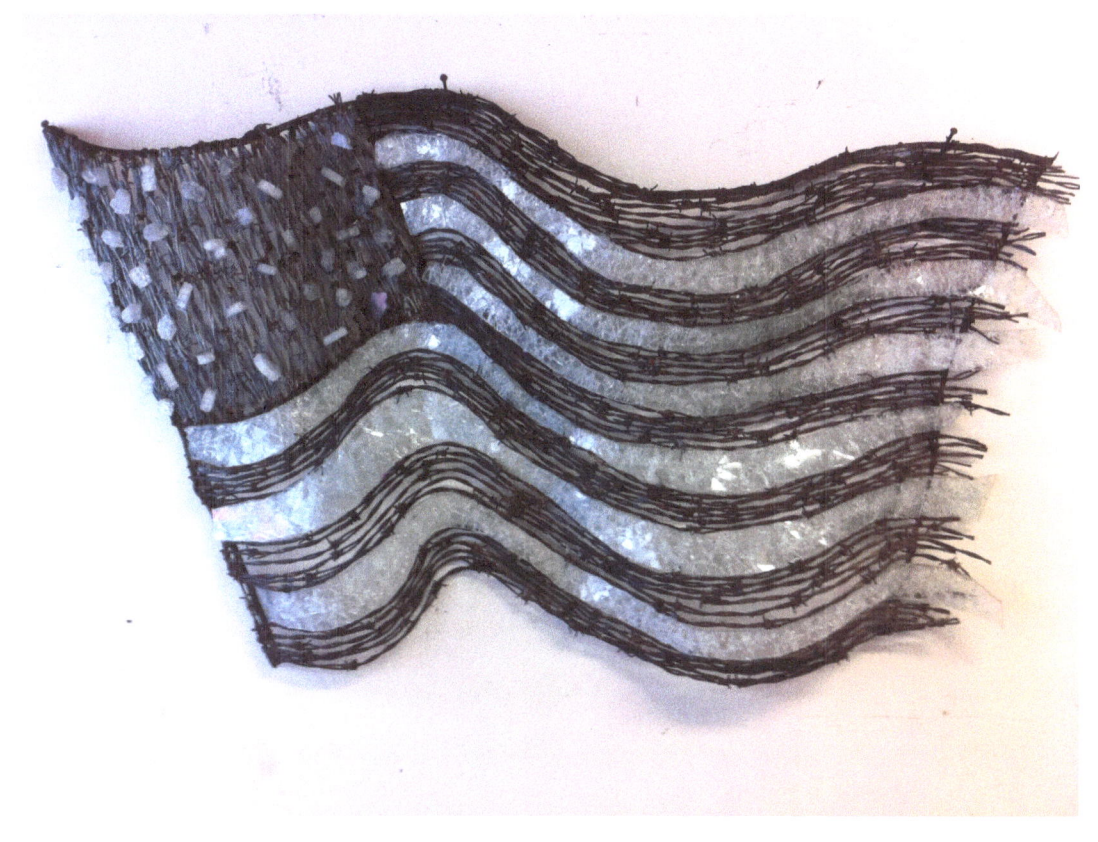

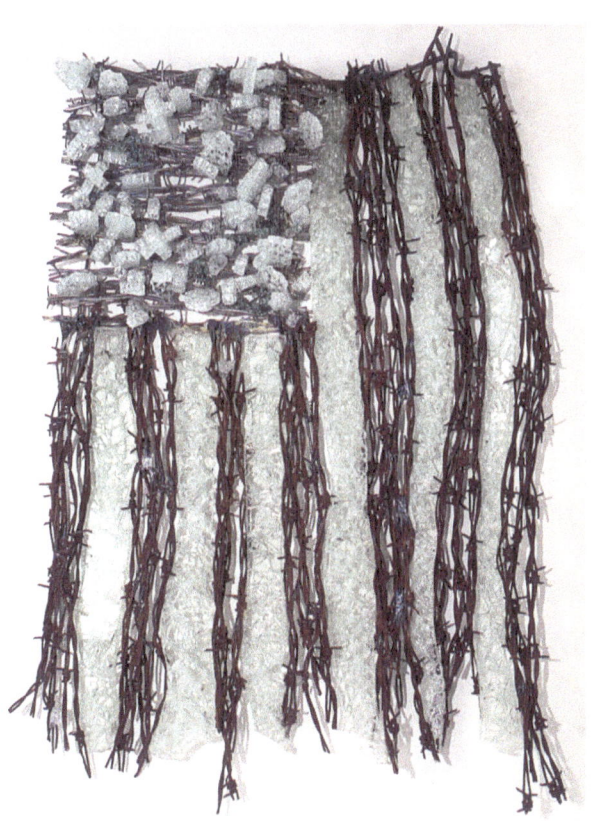

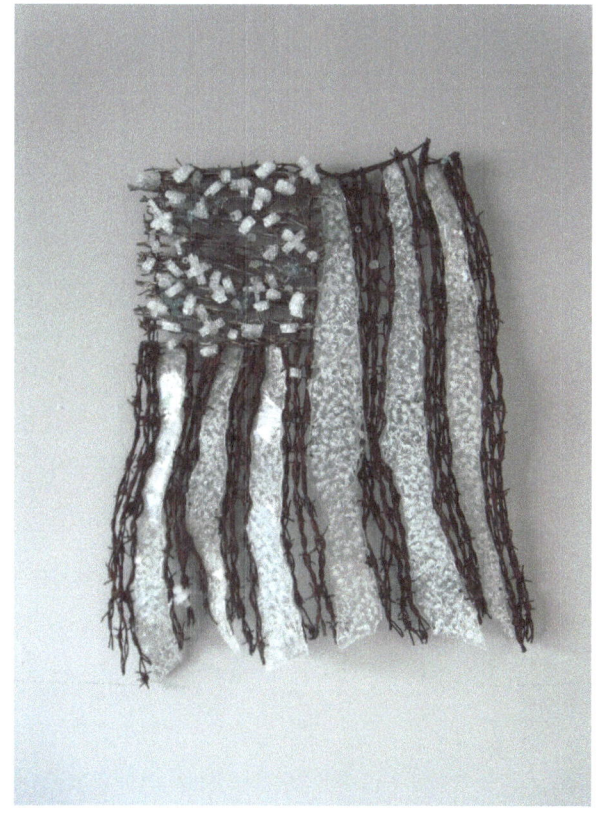

Top: American Flag Waving, approx. 34" x 28" x 10", broken glass & barbed wire
Left: American Flag, 29" x 25" x 6", broken glass & barbed wire
Right: American Flag, 28" x 24" x 5", broken glass & barbed wire

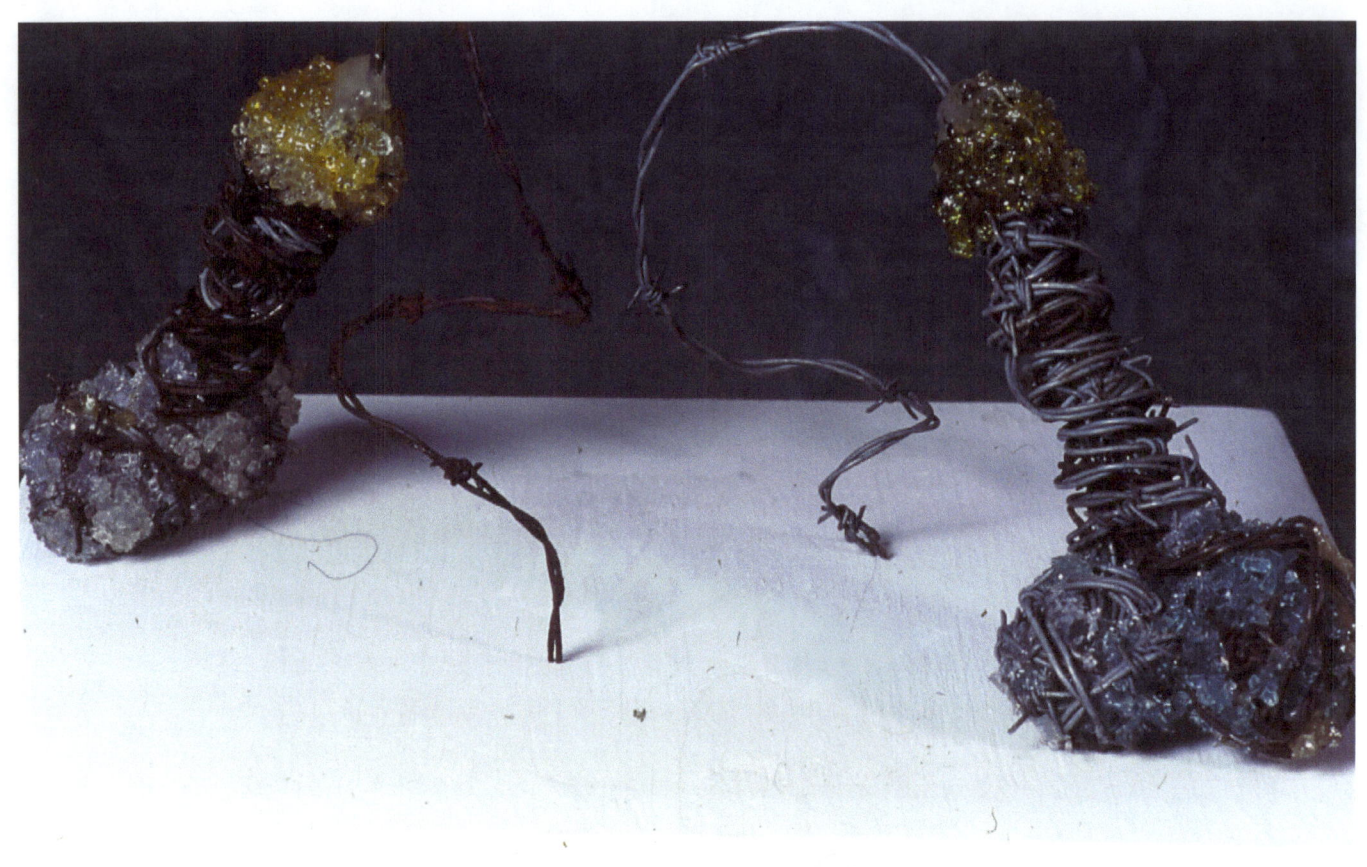

Dangerous Sex

The series Dangerous Sex started around 1995 as a concept. I was involved in community projects and people were dying of AIDS. I was thinking about materials and what to use in order to convey this concept. It occurred to me that broken glass and barbed wire were the answer.

This series of work is very important because of this discovery, and I continue to keep pushing the limits and boundaries of these materials.

Above Dangerous Sex #1 & 1A, 11" x 12" x 6"
broken glass & barbed wire

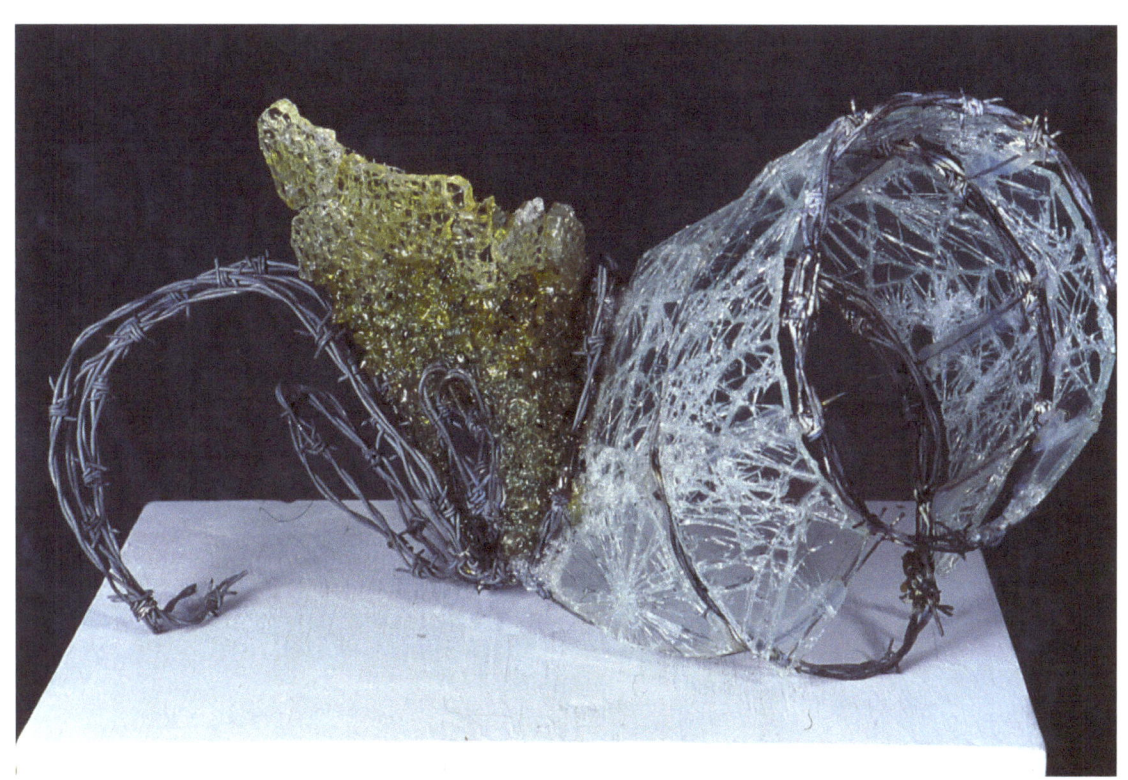

Above: Dangerous Sex #2, 24" x 20" x 12"
broken glass & barbed wire

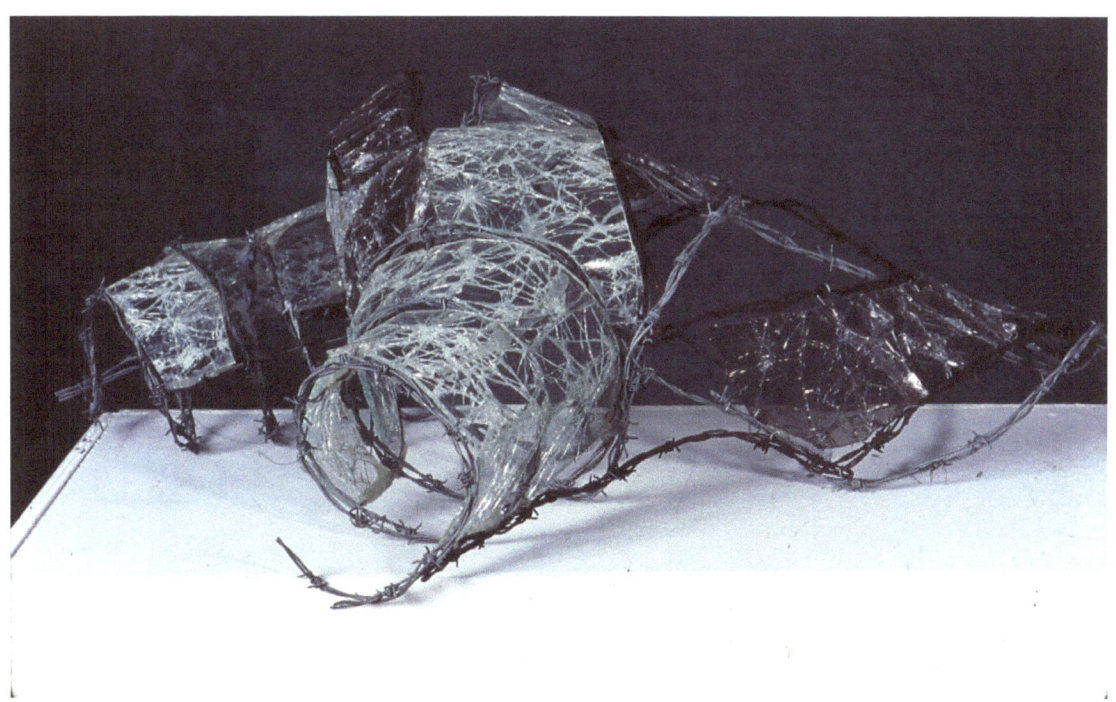

Above: Dangerous Sex #3, 40" x 30" x 16",
broken glass & barbed wire

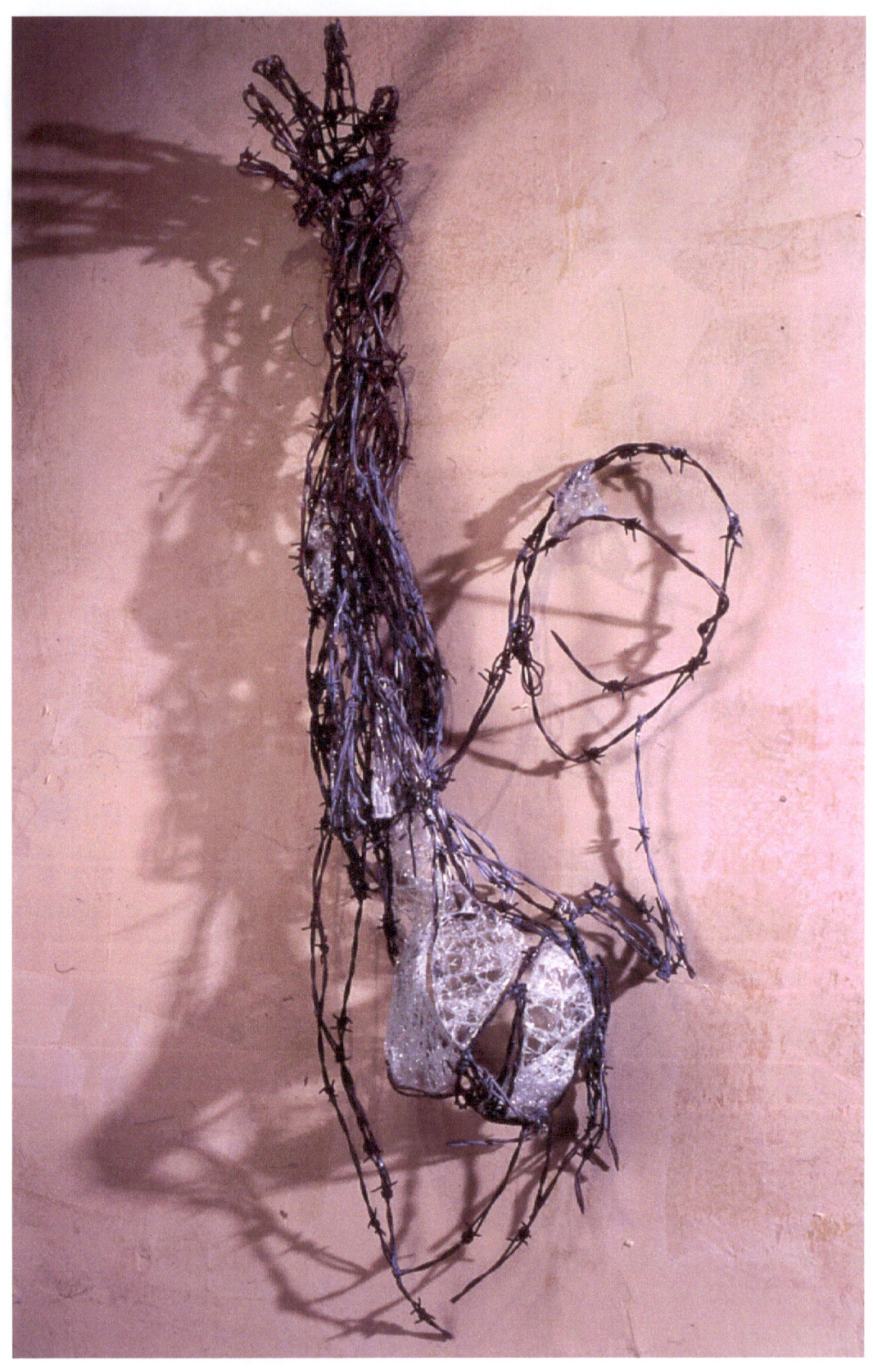

Dangerous Sex #4, 48" x 20" x 8"
broken glass & barbed wire

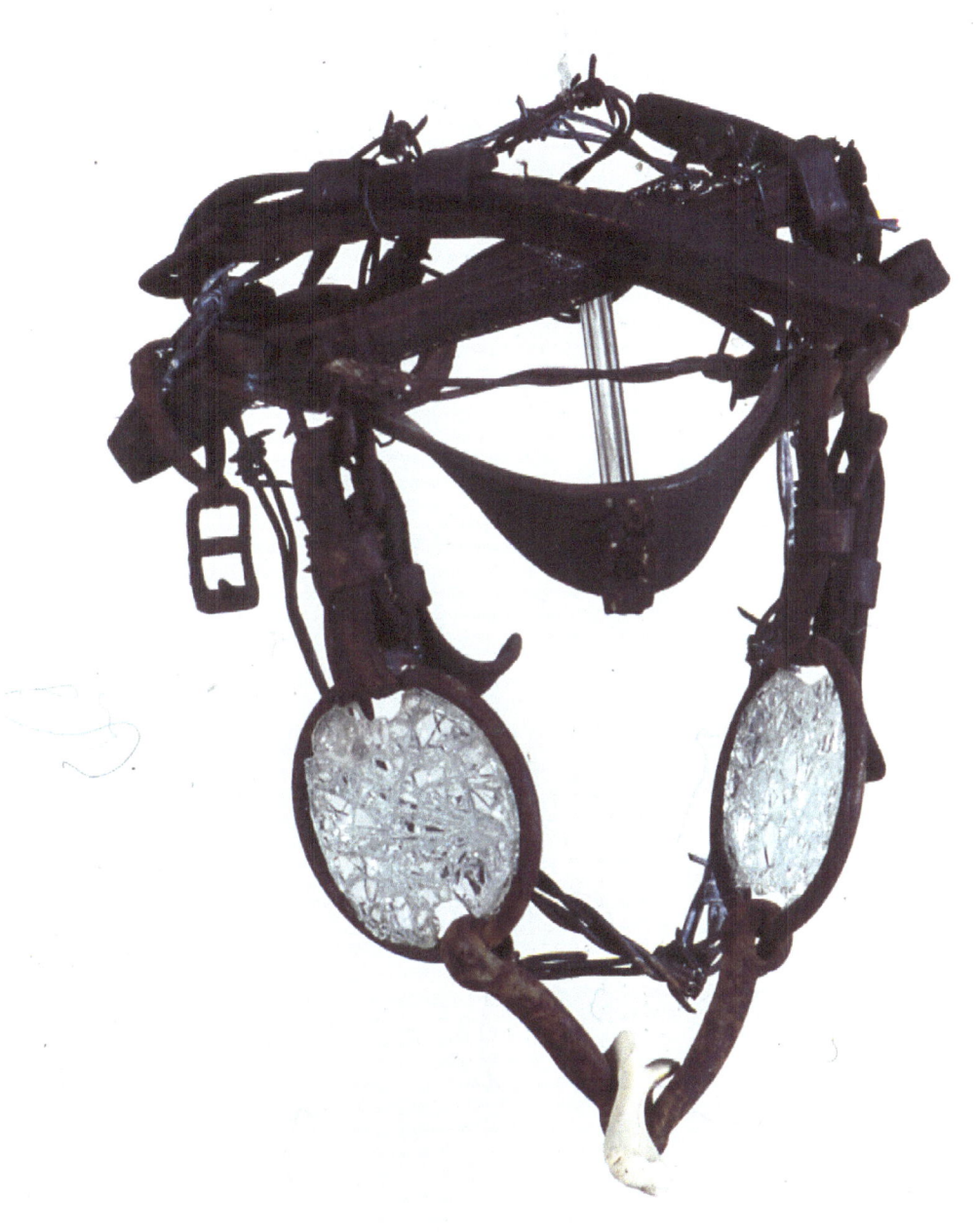

Bridal Mask, 13" x 13" x 10"
broken glass, barbed wire, & leather

Coupling

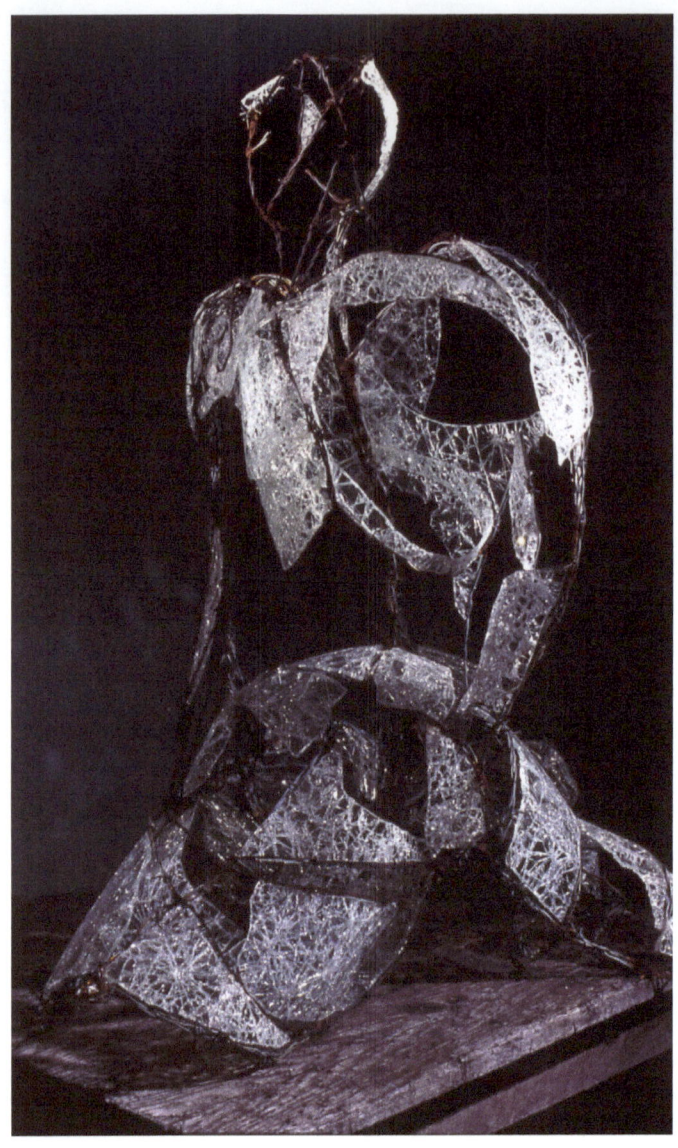

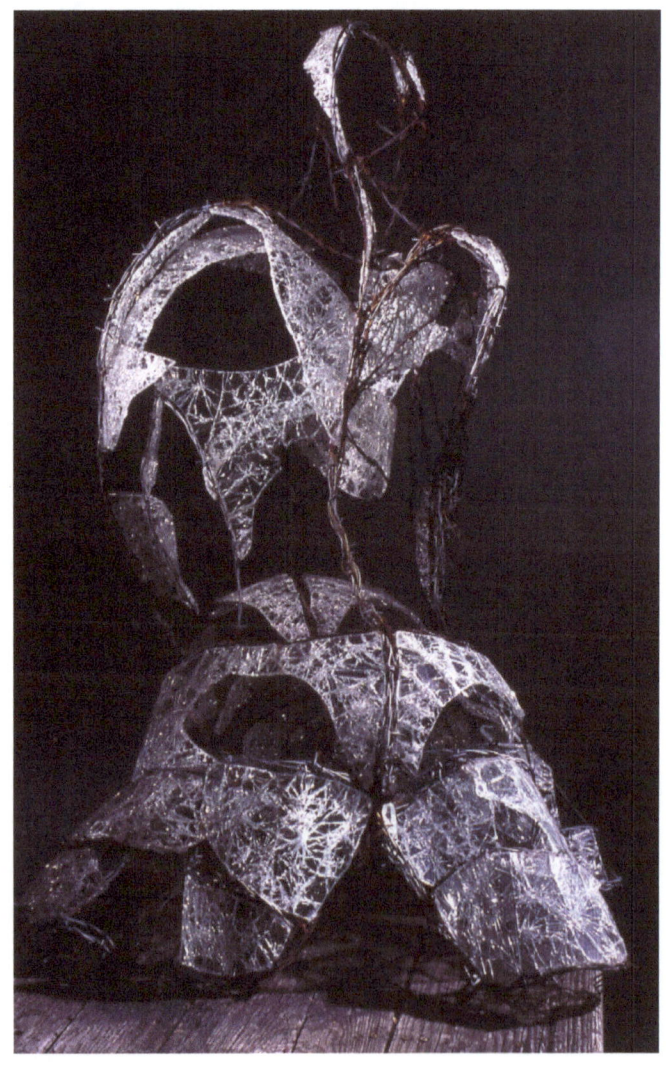

Below: Coupling (back)
75" x 50" x 30",
broken glass & barbed wire

Above: Coupling (front)
75" x 50" x 30",
broken glass & barbed wire

Maid In Form

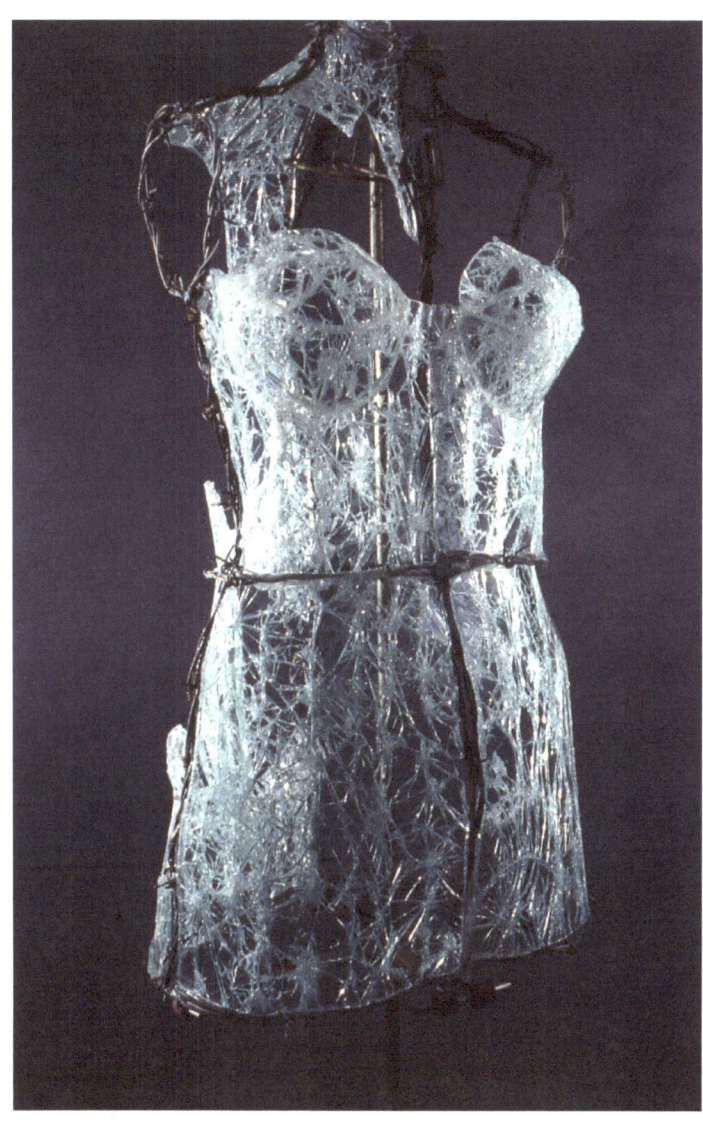

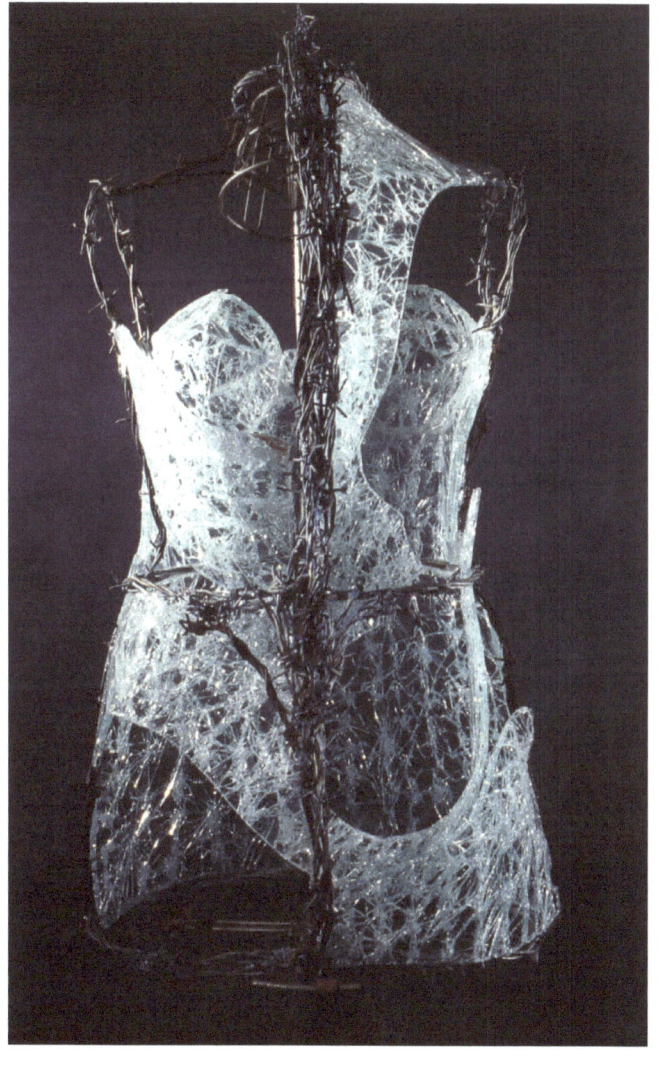

Below: Maid In Form (back)
36" x 18" x 12",
broken glass & barbed wire

Above: Maid In Form (front)
36" x 18" x 12",
broken glass & barbed wire

Double Faced Head/Mother & Son

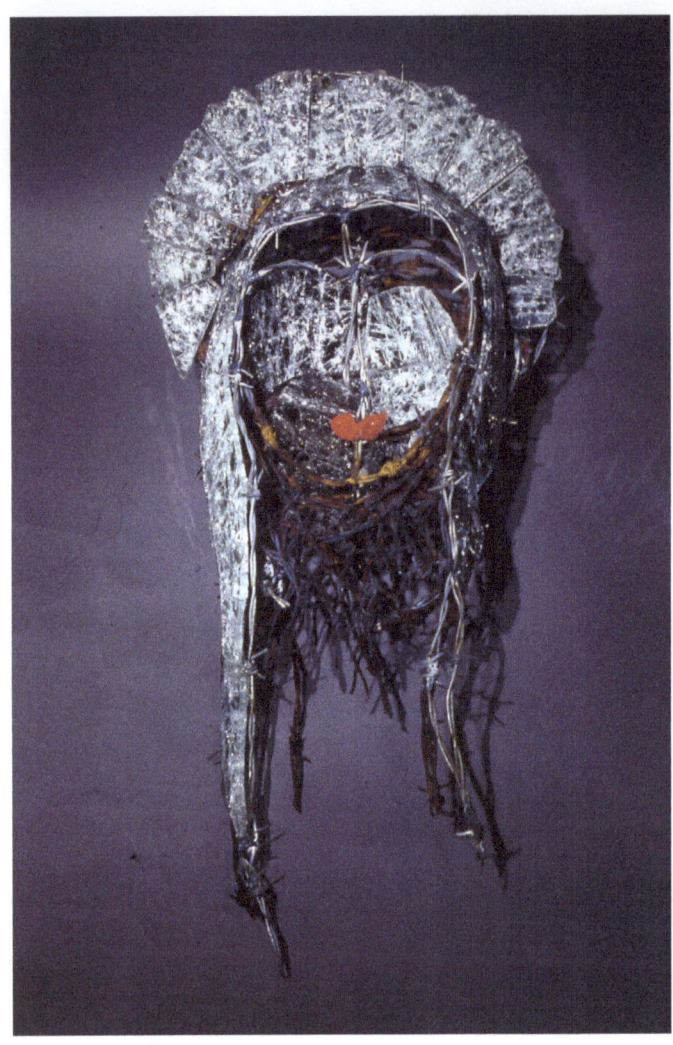

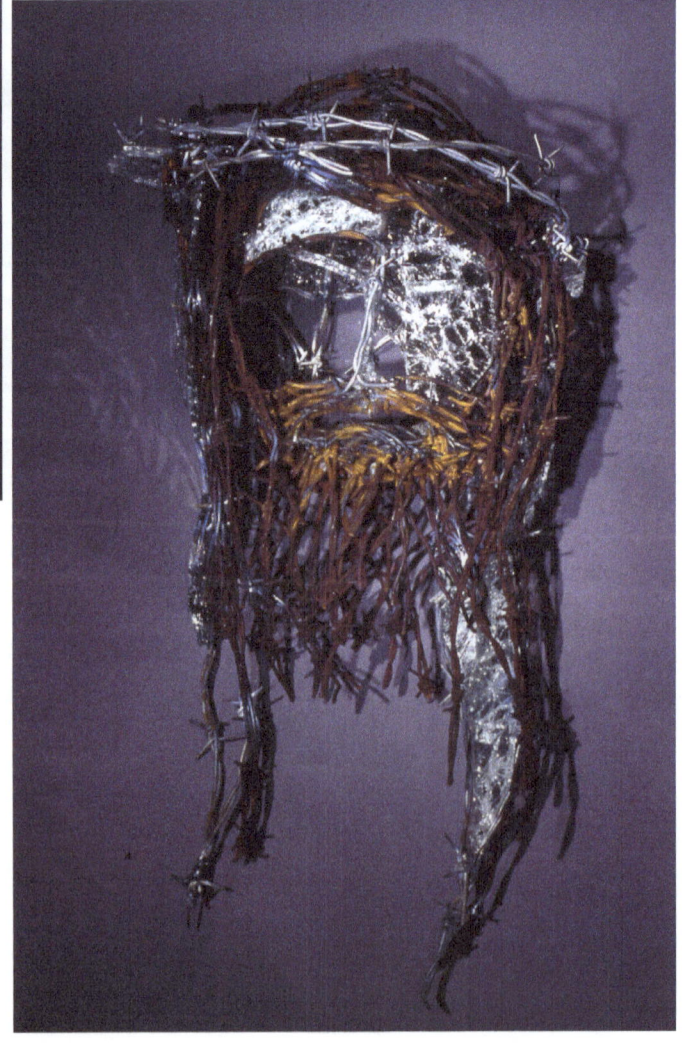

Below: Double Faced Head/Son
(one sculpture),
26" x 16" x 16",
broken glass & barbed wire

Above: Double Faced Head/Mother
(one sculpture),
26" x 16" x 16",
broken glass & barbed wire

Contact the Artist

Charlee Swanson

e-mail: charleeswanson@charleeswanson.com

website: www.charleeswanson.com

phone: (973) 222-0105

All Images and Work © Charlee Swanson
Special thanks to Danielle Quiroz for her creativity and help with the layout and design of this book.

www.ingramcontent.com/pod-product-compliance
Lightning Source LLC
Chambersburg PA
CBHW050407180526
45159CB00005B/2186